# GOSPEL *of* PEACE

*no more shame...no more fear!*

# GOSPEL of PEACE

*no more shame…no more fear!*

## DR. JAMES B. RICHARDS

Editorial note: Even at the cost of violating grammatical rules, we have chosen not to capitalize the name satan and related names.

## THE GOSPEL OF PEACE

Impact Ministries
3300 N. Broad Place SW
Huntsville, AL 35805
256.536.9402 • Fax: 256.536.4530

ISBN: 0-88368-487-X
Printed in the United States of America
© 1990 by Dr. James B. Richards

Whitaker House
30 Hunt Valley Circle
New Kensington, PA 15068
visit our web site: www.whitakerhouse.com

Library of Congress Cataloging-in-Publication Data

Richards, James B. (James Burton), 1951–
  The Gospel of peace / by James B. Richards.
     p. cm.
Includes bibliographical references.
  ISBN 0-88368-487-X (pbk. : alk. paper)
  1. Peace—Religious aspects—Christianity. 2. Bible. N.T.
Gospels—Criticism, interpretation, etc. 3. Jesus Christ—Person and
offices. I. Title.
  BT736.4 .R493 2002
  234—dc21                          2002005232

1 2 3 4 5 6 7 8 9 10 11 12 / 09 08 07 06 05 04 03 02

# Dedication

ೞ

This book is dedicated to Bobby C. Goode, my uncle. Thank you for being a role model, a friend, an example, and the only real father I ever knew.

Because you believed in me, I was able to believe in myself and come out of what would have been a disastrous lifestyle. In you, I saw high standards without rejection. You helped me to see God as a Father.

# About Impact Ministries

James B. Richards is president of Impact Ministries. This multifaceted, worldwide organization is pioneering a ministry movement that is making an impact on the entire world. Impact Ministries is committed to providing relevant, meaningful ministry to all nations, while equipping a new breed of leaders who are prepared to meet the challenges of the new millennium. To meet this worldwide demand, the ministry consists of:

1. Impact of Huntsville, a vibrant, cutting-edge, local church based in Huntsville, Alabama

2. Impact International Ministries, the missions arm of the organization that reaches the nations of the world

3. Impact International Fellowship of Ministers, a worldwide ministry base that trains, equips, and serves ministers to live their call while pioneering a new level of leadership

4. Impact International Publications, changing the way the world sees God through books, audio, video, and other published materials

5. Impact Ministries, which conducts life-changing seminars and outreaches in North America

6. Impact International School of Ministry, which provides one of the most unique ministry training opportunities in the world

For information on these and other services provided by Dr. Richards and his ministry team contact us at:

3300 N. Broad Place
Huntsville, AL 35805
256-536-9402
www.impactministries.com

## Other Books by James B. Richards

| | | |
|---|---|---|
| The Prayer Organizer | ISBN: 0-92474-801-X | 112 pages |
| Grace: The Power to Change | ISBN: 0-88368-730-5 | 192 pages |
| How to Stop the Pain | ISBN: 0-88368-722-4 | 208 pages |
| We Still Kiss | ISBN: 0-88368-752-6 | 208 pages |
| Escape from Codependent Christianity | ISBN: 0-92474-810-9 | 224 pages |
| Leadership That Builds People Vol. 1 | ISBN: 0-92474-806-0 | 160 pages |
| Leadership That Builds People Vol. 2 | ISBN: 0-92474-811-7 | 176 pages |
| Satan Unmasked | ISBN: 0-92474-812-5 | 176 pages |
| Taking the Limits Off God | ISBN: 0-92474-800-1 | 90 pages |
| My Church, My Family | ISBN: 0-92474-809-5 | 160 pages |
| Supernatural Ministry | ISBN: 0-92474-814-1 | 224 pages |

# Contents

ԥ

1. Experiencing the "Peace of God"........................9
2. A Relationship with God ...........................17
3. The Good News of Christ............................25
4. The Cross of Christ...................................31
5. Peace on Earth ........................................37
6. The Chastisement for "Our Peace" ...............45
7. Free from the Penalty ...............................55
8. The Exchange ........................................63
9. Faith-Righteousness.................................71
10. Faith to Faith.........................................81
11. Being Righteous We Have Peace....................89
12. The Covenant of Peace ............................101
13. The Love of God.....................................109
14. Good News Faith ...................................117
15. Sowing and Reaping ...............................125
16. A Relationship of Love.............................133
17. Discerning the Heart...............................139
18. Bringing Forth the Heart ..........................147
19. The Heart of the Father ............................155
20. Angry Preachers ....................................163
21. The Error of Balaam ...............................173

22. The Judgment of God ........................................................... 181
23. The Need for Peace ............................................................. 187
24. More than a State of Mind .................................................. 193
About the Author ...................................................................... 199
Bibliography ............................................................................. 203

# One

୫

# Experiencing the "Peace of God"

# One

## 𝒮

# Experiencing the "Peace of God"

*H*undreds of times in the Bible God, or an angel, tells man not to fear. When Jesus appeared to His disciples after His crucifixion, He said, "Fear not!" There should be no fear of God in the heart of a believer. There should be only a deep and powerful realization of being loved and accepted by God the Father, the Creator of the universe.

When fear is in a person's heart toward God, it is clear that the person in question does not really believe that God loves him with a perfect love. If there is fear, it is because that person is afraid of what God will do to him. He is afraid he will be hurt or rejected by God.

First John 4:18 is best expressed in *The Living Bible:*

> *We need have no fear of someone who loves us perfectly; his perfect love for us eliminates all dread of what he might do to us. If we are afraid, it is for fear of what he might do to us, and shows that we are not fully convinced that he really loves us.*

The earmark of the Christian who believes what Jesus did through His death, burial, and resurrection should be a life of confident acceptance that is permeated with peace. There should be no torment. There should be no nagging sense of guilt and rejection. There should be only peace.

Every religion in the world offers peace to man. Christianity is the only one, however, that delivers. For we are not a people that is attempting to achieve a state or status that will give us peace; we are a people that has been made right with God through the finished work of one Man, Christ Jesus. And because of His finished work, we have been granted peace with God.

Because not every Christian knows or believes this wonderful reality, not every Christian lives in a continual state of peace. Far too many Christians live in torment and turmoil, always fearful that things are not right between them and God.

My involvement in ministering to people in mental wards has proven this time and time again. I have repeatedly seen the emotionally unstable and the mentally tormented struggle with the fear of not being able to please God. The world is right when it says, "Religion will drive you crazy!" Religion is man's attempt to find peace with God. Christianity, on the other hand, is man's accepting peace with God through the Lord Jesus Christ.

A great percentage of people in mental hospitals feel they have done something that is beyond God's ability to forgive. They are awaiting judgment from an angry God. Many times they have no idea what they could have done; they just have a sense of fear and impending judgment. This is what the Bible calls condemnation, or the expectation of damnation and judgment. In Christ. though, we are free from condemnation!

What is so sad is that this portrait of fearful people also describes many of the faithful who sit in church every Sunday. Fear seems to be the motivating factor in the lives of many Christians. Where would these people get such an idea about God? How could someone become so afraid of God that he would end up in a metal institution or chronically fearful and depressed? Who represented God so negatively that an entire world is turned off? It has not been some force outside the church that has so destroyed the reputation of God. It has not been some evil, demonic group. Unfortunately, it has been the voices of well-meaning people within the church.

Fear has been passed down from generation to generation in the church. From the earliest of times, the church has struggled with believing the truth about the finished work of Jesus. This failure to believe the truth has been the root of the fear, anxiety, and sometimes outright meanness of the church down through the ages.

When Isaiah prophesied about the great work of the cross, he also prophesied, *"Who has believed our report?"* (Isaiah 53:1 NKJV). There is a report about God that is so good, so freeing, so loving, so kind, so merciful, and so generous that man refuses to believe it.

Those who reject this wonderful report either spend a lifetime trying to please God or ultimately walk away from God. In my years of ministering on the streets, more people were angry at God because of the unbelieving report they heard in church than for any other reason.

In his introduction to the book of Galatians in *The Message*, Eugene H. Peterson says, "When men and women get their hands on religion, one of the first things they often do is turn it into an instrument for controlling others, either putting or keeping them in their place." This control seems to have become the goal of the church. Rather than setting people free with the good news about Jesus, they use it as a way to bring people under their control.

Early in Christian history there arose those who would pervert the Gospel. There were those who followed Paul around and proclaimed, "Believe on Jesus! He is the Messiah. He is the way of salvation. But the way of righteousness is works of the law." The deceit in this message is subtle. It is obvious that God has called us to live a righteous life. It is obvious that righteousness should be the fruit of being a Christian. So it would seem only logical to accept this message. However, what you believe about righteousness is really what you believe about how you relate to God.

If keeping the law is our basis for righteousness, then it is also the basis for receiving the promises of God. It is the basis of getting our prayers answered. It is the basis of God's protection. If keeping the law is the basis of righteousness, then our ability to have peace is determined by our ability to keep the law. Ultimately, keeping the law becomes our basis for salvation.

While proclaiming belief in Jesus as the way of salvation in one breath, we have totally excluded Jesus in the next breath. Of course, none of us denies Jesus as Lord. In experience, however, we look to our performance to provide everything that Jesus died to provide. Intellectually and theologically, Jesus is still the center of our faith, but emotionally and functionally, *we* have become the center of our faith.

Romans 8:5–8 in *The Message* says it this way:

> *Those who think they can do it on their own end up obsessed with measuring their own moral muscle but never get around to exercising it in real life. Those who*

*trust God's action in them find that God's Spirit is in them—living and breathing God! Obsession with self in these matters is a dead end; attention to God leads us out into the open, into a spacious, free life. Focusing on the self is the opposite of focusing on God. Anyone completely absorbed in self ignores God, ends up thinking more about self than God. That person ignores who God is and what he is doing. And God isn't pleased at being ignored.*

This self-obsession is not the product of a person who desires to reject God. Rather, this is the person who is trying to please God by his own efforts. This is the person who has ignorantly rejected the finished work of Jesus and has become obsessed with earning righteousness by his performance; thus he has an obsession with self.

Every letter Paul wrote was aimed at bringing believers back to the finished work of Jesus. One by one, church by church, city after city, many believers forgot the message and were seduced by others into returning to their own performance as their source of righteousness and ultimately their source of peace with God. They just would not believe the report about Jesus.

In the book of Galatians, Paul pointed out the motivation of those who pervert the Gospel: control! Leaders who don't trust Jesus don't believe the Gospel will work by its own power. Because they themselves do not believe in the power of the Gospel, they feel it is their job to control you, to "put you in your place."

What makes this so undetectable is the motive. Many of the most destructive forces in the church are people with good motives. The most dangerous person is the one who has a deep passion to help people but who does not believe in the power of the Gospel to produce change. Instead of proclaiming the finished work of the Lord Jesus and entrusting the people to the work of the Holy Spirit, that person will resort to carnal methods of control. When people are controlled, it appears that they have changed. So the deep motive to help people justifies the desire to control.

The main tool for control is fear. If you are not confident in your relationship with God, you will have fear. Fear will rob you of confidence. It will restrict you. It will make you angry. It will make you emotionally unstable. Fear will strip you of the new identity you have in Jesus. It will leave you stripped of the God-ordained dignity and worth that belong to you as a priest and a king. It will make you feel the need for an intercessor.

The intercessor who will come between you and God will not be the Lord Jesus, however. After all, you have rejected the peace He gives for the peace that someone else is offering. Instead, this intercessor will be someone who offers to show you the way—the formula. It will be someone who will know all the rules and requirements for staying right with God. You will be saved but never secure. Your sin will be forgiven but never forgotten. You will have the promises but never the qualification to receive them. You will be given the family name but never the family inheritance. You will forever strive to attain what Jesus has freely given. You will be offered peace but never have peacefulness.

This is not the plan of God for you. God desires for you to know and experience His great love, acceptance, and peace. But you must believe the report God gives about the finished work of Jesus. It is a good report. It is a report of peace!

# Two

### &

# A Relationship
# with God

# Two

## ଈ

# A Relationship with God

*T*he ultimate goal of the Gospel is a loving, meaningful relationship with God. Until people understand
this goal, they will pervert the process. Because we
fail to realize what God desires, we spend much of our time
and effort pursuing an entirely different goal than that which
God desires.

Jesus did not come to build an army. He came to recover
a family. Through His work we are adopted, not inducted.
Adoption is acceptance into a family. Induction is enlistment
into an army. God is our Father, not our general. Although Jesus
is our Lord, He is also our Elder Brother. The ultimate goal of
God is not a labor force or a warring force; it is a family.

God wants us as His sons and daughters. He wants us to
be a part of His family. He wants our involvement. He wants
a relationship with us. Therefore, He initiated the plan that
could bring all of this about. He dealt with the one thing that
stood between us and Him: sin!

Sin had separated man from God. Sin had created a bridge
that we could not cross. Sin introduced the one thing that

would keep us from loving, trusting, or being involved with God. It began to reign with Adam, and it has continued until this very day.

Genesis gives us some insight into the way sin affected man's relationship with God. Genesis 3:8 is one of the saddest verses in all the Bible.

> *And they heard the voice of the LORD God walking in the garden in the cool of the day: and Adam and his wife hid themselves from the presence of the LORD God amongst the trees of the garden.*

Just as God had initiated this whole plan of man, just as He had initiated every aspect of Creation, just as He had initiated a relationship with man to start with, this day He initiated a visit with Adam. But for the first time, man didn't respond. He hid from God. From that day until the present, man has continued to run from the invitation of God. Man has refused to draw near and experience God.

Genesis 3:9 says, *"And the LORD God called unto Adam, and said unto him, Where art thou?"* There is every indication from the original language that when God called, it meant He "called to make peace." God wanted peace. Adam assumed God called for judgment. That assumption is perpetuated in fearful men to this day.

Unfortunately, this fear of God is not experienced exclusively among the lost. Even after people are saved, they have reservations about intimacy with God. Among believers, there is a lack of confidence concerning God's desire to be intimate with us. There is a low-level, nagging fear in most people. They do not really believe that they are acceptable to God.

We have the illusion that we are trying to get holy enough to have involvement with God. But our attempt to be made acceptable is like Adam's. Adam had always been naked before God. Now Adam, through his newfound abilities, determined that God should not see him naked. So Adam made a covering out of fig leaves. Thus when God came looking for Adam in the Garden, Adam didn't think he could stand before God, and he did what he thought would make him acceptable. Adam, like us, missed the point. If God did not want to fellowship with Adam, He would not have come to the Garden looking for him.

Our fears, like Adam's, affect our behavior so dramatically that we cannot have meaningful involvement with God. We do not accept the reality that God pursued us in Jesus. He made us acceptable. He wants a relationship so much that He has done everything to make this relationship possible.

Meaningful relationships are the product of love, trust, and personal involvement. Relationships grow to the extent that each of these factors is present. When there is no love, trust, and personal involvement, it is not a relationship. At best, it might be considered an arrangement or a "working relationship." It is not a personal, family relationship.

We need time with God in order to develop and experience these factors. When you spend time with someone who is kind to you, you grow in your trust for him. All positive involvement is part of developing the relationship. However, you will not spend time with someone if you do not realize that he accepts you. You will never have the opportunity to experience God until the issue of peace is resolved.

The one element that hinders a real relationship more than anything else is fear. Fear breeds all sorts of negative emotions and actions. It is the root of deceit. You can never be honest with someone when you fear what he will do to you or how he will respond. You can never be real. You are too busy trying to cover your faults to develop a relationship.

This all began in the Garden. Man started running and has never stopped, because we are afraid of God. We don't really believe how God feels about us. We have not allowed love to deliver us from the power of fear.

There is a real possibility that the sin nature is not necessarily a nature that just craves sin. There is every indication that the essence of the sin nature is fear. Fear was the first emotion mankind displayed after Adam ate of the Tree of Knowledge of Good and Evil. It was fear that made Adam hide from God. It is fear that makes us turn to sinful actions instead of trusting God.

Fear and unbelief go hand in hand. Where there is one, there is always the other. Because we are afraid of God, we do not trust Him. Because we do not trust Him, we do not come to Him to receive strength and help in our time of need. We do not believe He will really give us the promises He has made, because we are afraid.

What do we fear? We are afraid that we are unacceptable to God, that He does not approve of us. We are afraid that we do not measure up and that He will find fault in us and punish us. We are afraid because we do not believe that we are righteous.

This fear prevents us from having an open, honest relationship with God. It keeps us from all honest and open communication. It destroys all possibility of knowing God. It makes us emotionally unstable. It brings all matter of torment into our lives. There is an endless list of the negative effects of fear.

Some might say, "I thought you were supposed to fear God." In the King James Version, numerous Scriptures tell us the value of having the fear of God. Let's take a closer look at the admonition to fear God.

On the one hand, you have Scriptures that tell you to fear God. On the other, God often begins speaking with the words, "Fear not." When there are obvious contradictions like this, I have found that there is usually something I am not understanding.

First John 4:18 tells us, *"Perfect love casts out fear"* (NKJV). This means that fear and love cannot coexist. If I grow in the love of God, the fear of God will diminish in my life. I know God is love. I know God wants me to experience His love. But what about the fear of God?

When Jesus was tempted, He quoted an Old Testament Scripture: *"Then saith Jesus unto him, Get thee hence, Satan: for it is written, Thou shalt worship the Lord thy God, and him only shalt thou serve"* (Matthew 4:10). Jesus was quoting from Deuteronomy 6:13, where it says, *"Thou shalt fear the LORD thy God, and serve him, and shalt swear by his name."* Jesus translated the word *"fear"* as *"worship."*

Actually, the word for *fear* in the Old Testament is better understood as "awe, respect, and love that produces worship." We should have an awe of God that produces worship, not fear. God does not want you to be afraid of Him.

To be afraid of God would contradict all we know about Jesus, His life, and His ministry. It makes an honest relationship impossible. It prevents everything that Jesus came to establish. He came to restore us to the Father. He brought about our adoption into the family of God.

The religious leaders of Jesus' day had completely misrepresented God. They had portrayed God as hard and judgmental. They had perverted the meaning and purpose of the law. They had put God completely out of reach of the people.

Jesus came and properly represented God to the world. He said, "If you've seen Me, you've seen the Father." (See John 14:9.) Hebrews 1:3 in *The New International Version* says that Jesus was the exact representation of God. Jesus was approachable. He was merciful. He was open. He was relationship-oriented. This was the complete opposite of the God represented by the Jewish leaders and is somewhat contrary to the God the church has frequently presented.

Jesus showed us God so that we could have boldness to enter into a meaningful relationship with Him. God desires our presence. He desires our hearts. He wants a relationship with us.

Three

&

# The Good News
# of Christ

*Three*

### ❧

# *The Good News of Christ*

When Jesus appeared on the scene, He preached the Gospel of the kingdom of God. The word *gospel* simply means "good news." It is not complicated. Everything Jesus preached was good news. When the masses were healed, it was because they had heard good news. When there were miracles, it was because the people had heard good news. When people turned from their sins, it was because they had heard good news.

The religious leaders of the day preached to the people, but they never brought them good news about God; they always brought bad news. They didn't set people free; they loaded them down with more rules and regulations. They made the people afraid of God. They caused the people to view God as mean, hard, and judgmental. Because they never preached good news, they never saw good results.

When people are afraid of God, they not only fail to establish a relationship with Him, but they also never have real productivity in their lives. In Jesus' parable about the talents, the man who had only one talent refused to utilize that talent because he was afraid of God. Fear binds, destroys, and restricts.

Despite the best attempts of the religious leaders of that day, what they had was not working. It did not set people free; it bound them. They all knew about God, but they did not know the Good News about God. The Pharisees had burdened the people with negatives—law and works—but they did not lift one finger to lighten their load.

Jesus came reading the same Scriptures, praying to the same God, but proclaiming good things and good news. It rang in my heart like a bell of freedom: Jesus preached good news to the people. By His preaching the Good News, their faith was established, their hunger for God was heightened, and their trust for the One who had once seemed so far away and unconcerned was revived. When they found out God was a good God, miracles happened.

Galatians 1:8 says, *"But though we, or an angel from heaven, preach any other gospel unto you than that which we have preached unto you, let him be accursed."* We have departed from the Good News. Our religious system of today is built on the premise of an angry God. When people go to church, they are often "beaten" instead of fed. I was as guilty as any other minister. One day while reading these words in Galatians, the revelation exploded in my heart: "If it is not good news, it is not Gospel."

At one time, I was winning a few hundred people per year to the Lord. Then God spoke to me and said, "When you start preaching the Gospel, you will really do something for Me." I was insulted. "What do You mean, 'When I start preaching the Gospel'?" I thought I was preaching the Gospel. I began to look at what I was telling people. It was mostly bad news. When people presented their problems to me, I was not mean or condemning, but I did not have a sure word that was always good. I did not have a word that always gave freedom. I did not have good news. Paul said in Romans 1:16, *"For I am not ashamed of the gospel* [the Good News] *of Christ: for it is the power of God unto salvation to every one that believeth."* The good news of Jesus is the power of God. Without good news, there is no power.

The word *salvation* comes from the Greek word *sozo. Sozo* is more than the new birth. It means healing, protection, deliverance, safety, and a host of other good things. If I do not preach the Good News, the power of God cannot come and bring salvation (*sozo*) into the lives of hurting people.

The Good News is not life for everyone—only for those who believe it. When Jesus began His public ministry, He proclaimed the purpose for which the Spirit of the Lord was upon Him—to preach good news (Luke 4:18). He had good news for the poor, the brokenhearted, the captives, the blind, and the bruised. The Good News is found in Luke 4:19: *"To preach the acceptable year of the Lord."* What could He possibly have meant by that?

*"The acceptable year of the Lord"* is the Year of Jubilee. Every fifty years all debts were canceled. Regardless of how legitimate a debt might be, it was canceled. The individual was free from the debt without any effort or merit on his part. The debt was canceled. By the debt being canceled, the penalty of the debt was also canceled. Every good Jew knew the penalty for breaking the law was the curse, as described in the old covenant. When those curses came, he knew he deserved it. He could in no way hold God responsible for the curse of the law. But to all those curses—poverty, brokenheartedness, captivity, blindness, and bruising—Jesus was saying, "The debt is now canceled." That is the Good News to those in need. The debt of the law is canceled. You can now be free from the penalty of your sin.

Jesus repeatedly proved that this applied to the forgiveness of sins as well as to the curse of the law. The Pharisees never believed that, and they never partook of it. They may have loved God, but they were offended by the Good News. Despite what we might think, some of those Pharisees had something in their hearts for God. It may have been twisted and perverted, but they must have wanted God very much in order to live the rigid lifestyle they lived.

In the *Archko Volume,* the Pharisees revealed some of their fears concerning Jesus' message. They were afraid that when the people believed in the Good News, they would fall into sin. They failed to understand that the law affects the outer man, while mercy and love affect the inner man. Jesus' message of forgiveness was accused of promoting a loose and lascivious lifestyle.

Contrary to this unfounded belief, the Good News that Jesus preached caused people to fall in love with God. It caused people to trust the God they had grown to dread. It caused them to draw near to the One from whom they had been hiding. It caused them to come out of the stronghold of sin by entering into intimacy with God.

Jesus' preaching of the Good News succeeded where law had failed. By His preaching and demonstrating the goodness of God, the people were able to respond properly. The natural response to goodness is appreciation, thanksgiving, commitment, and relationship. Thus, we see the reality that the Gospel (Good News) is the power of God unto salvation, healing, deliverance, and every other promise that God has made.

# Four

&

# The Cross of Christ

*Four*

&

# The Cross of Christ

*For I determined not to know any thing among you, save Jesus*
*Christ, and him crucified. And I was with you in weakness,*
*and in fear, and in much trembling. And my speech and my*
*preaching was not with enticing words of man's wisdom, but*
*in demonstration of the Spirit and of power: that your faith*
*should not stand in the wisdom of men, but in*
*the power of God.*
*—1 Corinthians 2:2–5*

*T*hese words haunted me for years. What did this really mean? Did Paul preach only a salvation (born-again experience) message? Did he preach only about the cross and nothing else? I had to know what this meant.

Sometimes the simple and the obvious is the most difficult to grasp. As I developed my understanding of the Word of God, I came to realize that all understanding, all revelation, all that God has done for us can be understood only in the finished work of the cross. I realized the Gospel was understood only in the death, burial, and resurrection of the Lord Jesus.

The rest of the New Testament teaching simply explains and points back to what happened on the cross. The cross is the basis of the entire new covenant. It is the basis of my relationship with God. It is the basis of all of Christianity. All truth has its basis in the cross. Any message that is not consistent with what Jesus accomplished at the cross is simply not true.

Hebrews 1:1–2 says,

> *God, who at sundry times and in divers manners spake in time past unto the fathers by the prophets, hath in these last days spoken unto us by his Son, whom he hath appointed heir of all things, by whom also he made the worlds.*

Prior to the cross, God had spoken in many different ways, through many different people, in many different situations. Now, however, He has said all He has to say in the Son— specifically, in the death, burial, and resurrection of His Son. God has no other message. What happened at the cross is the basis of the Good News that God has for the world.

The cross must become my focal point for understanding, interpreting, and judging truth. In other words, anything I find in the entire Bible must pass the test of the cross. Is it consistent with what Jesus accomplished on the cross? Or does it contradict the cross? A failure to interpret doctrine in light of the finished work of the cross has been the major cause of confusion and contradictory teachings.

In our failure to base our entire belief system on the cross, we have erroneously looked back to the old covenant to relate to God. Because the message of the cross seems too good to be true, we have, in our unbelief, looked other places to know and experience God.

At the cross, Jesus paid the price for sin and delivered us from the curse of the law. Yet we still look to the law and assume that our standard of conduct will protect us from the curse. At the cross, Jesus was chastened so that we could have peace. In our unbelief, we live in expectancy of God chastening us. At the cross, Jesus was bruised with sickness so we could have healing. But again we look to some stipulation of the law to give us healing. At the cross, Jesus conquered sin. We try to conquer it in our own strength. At the cross, Jesus conquered death by the Resurrection and obtained righteousness, yet we still try to obtain righteousness by our own works. We have abandoned the cross.

Although the cross is the central message of the Gospel, we have failed to embrace it as Paul and the early church did. We have verbally acknowledged it as the apex of Christianity, but in reality our doctrine and practical application totally deny the cross. Rather than our Christianity revolving around and depending on the finished work of the cross, it depends on us. We are more aware of our works than we are of His work. We erroneously place ourselves, instead of Jesus and His finished work, at the center of our relationship with God.

In short, we will never experience the power of God until our faith stands in the cross instead of the wisdom of men. The simple realities of the cross are the basis for real Bible faith. To live by faith is to live dependent on, trusting in, adhering to, and deriving power from what Jesus did at the cross. All else is simply vain imaginations.

Our faith as Christians is obviously in the person of Jesus. Yet there is no separating who Jesus is from what He has done. There is no operation of faith apart from faith in His finished work. This is the basis for faith. Faith (trust) based on anything else is vanity. It is a denial of the cross of Christ.

This causes us to ask some hard questions of ourselves. Do we really even know what Jesus accomplished at the cross? If so, do we really believe it? Has the cross of Christ become the pivotal point around which our lives revolve, or is it just an addendum to the Old Testament?

Paul said this in 1 Corinthians 1:17: *"For Christ sent me...to preach the gospel: not with wisdom of words, lest the cross of Christ should be made of none effect."* We preach Christ, but we don't preach the cross of Christ—at least not the way Paul and the early church understood it. For that reason, we don't see the same results he saw.

Some of the deepest, most profound, most challenging sermons I have ever heard were not based on the cross. They had a show of wisdom. They were logical. They were about Jesus. They were about loyalty and commitment to Jesus as a person. Yet, in the maze of man's wisdom, those messages never brought one to the place where his confidence before God was based on what Jesus accomplished in His death, burial, and resurrection.

On the other hand, I have heard many heart-moving messages of the cross. I have wept because I was so stirred. Yet, when I walked away and reflected on what I had heard, I realized it never acknowledged the provisions that God made through the cross.

Today I have so committed myself to the message of the cross that I can understand something in the Bible only when I understand it in light of the cross. If what I believe is not consistent with the cross, I must realize that I do not yet understand it. I am only beginning to understand why Paul preached nothing but Jesus and Him crucified.

# Five

છ

# Peace on Earth

# Five

## ಬಿ

# Peace on Earth

*J*esus is the Prince of Peace. God the Father is identified as the God of Peace. The fruit of the Spirit is peace. We are told that we should allow the peace of God to rule in our hearts. Why then are so few Christians experiencing peace?

Instead of being filled with peace, the Christian life for many is brimming with fear, guilt, and condemnation. They should be experiencing freedom from these negative emotions. It seems, however, that quite the opposite is true. Many Christians feel afraid and insecure. They feel that they are continually failing to measure up. According to one study, evangelical Christians have incredibly low self-worth. The legalistic, unscriptural tendency to reject righteousness as a free gift creates guilt and low self-worth in the presence of a holy God.

Low self-worth among Christians is the product of fear in our relationship with God. Instead of accepting and believing the truth about our new identity in Jesus, instead of believing what God has made us to be, we are trying to become what we think God would have us to be.

We are like Adam. God had created Adam in His own likeness and image. Then Satan came along and told Adam, "If you'll do this, you will be like God." Adam already was like God, but he fell because he simply did not believe it. In the same way, we have been made righteous in Jesus. The tempter says to us, "If you will do this, it will make you become like Jesus." We are like Jesus already; yet we fall into his trap because we just don't believe it. So instead of what we *do* stemming from who we are, we try to make who we are the *product* of what we do.

If I think I must become something to be acceptable to God, then I must also believe that I am not acceptable to God in my present state. Hence, low self-worth, rejection, and fear rule in my heart instead of peace. I find myself striving instead of resting, doubting instead of believing.

Colossians 3:15 tells us, *"And let the peace of God rule in your hearts, to the which also ye are called in one body; and be ye thankful."* My heart should always be ruled by peace. There should never be a time when another emotion is allowed to dominate my thoughts, feelings, and actions.

But the truth is, if I believe what mainstream Christianity teaches about God, I will never be at peace. I will never have an abiding peace that dominates my every decision and thought. I will, instead, live in dread and fear of what God might do to me. I will forever be striving to measure up to the standards of behavior imposed on me by the religious system.

Jesus came to establish peace. As He was preparing to leave earth, He said, *"Peace I leave with you, my peace I give unto you: not as the world giveth, give I unto you. Let not your heart be troubled, neither let it be afraid"* (John 14:27). According to Colossians 3:15, I must allow peace to rule my heart. His perfect peace will protect me from fear and guard my heart from trouble. Isaiah 26:3 promises, *"You will keep him in perfect peace, whose mind is stayed on You, because he trusts in You"* (NKJV).

As with all my beliefs, I must look back to the cross to find the basis for my peace with God. I do not want a false peace that is not based on reality. I do not want to look to myself and my performance to determine my level of peace. I want to look to the work of Jesus. I want a peace that has its foundation in what He has done for me.

When Jesus was born, the angels appeared to the shepherds in the countryside around Bethlehem. Their announcement of the birth of our Savior and Lord was magnificent. There was joy in heaven that could not be contained.

> *And the angel said unto them, Fear not: for, behold, I bring you good tidings of great joy, which shall be to all people. For unto you is born this day in the city of David a Saviour, which is Christ the Lord....And suddenly there was with the angel a multitude of the heavenly host praising God, and saying, Glory to God in the highest, and on earth peace, good will toward men.*
> (Luke 2:10–11, 13–14)

This announcement was so glorious that it could not be contained in heaven. There was good news coming to man from God. This would be the most valuable announcement God had ever made to fallen man. For the first time since Adam tried to run from God's presence in the Garden, there was going to be peace between God and man.

Man had already experienced miracles. He had seen healings. Actually, every miracle of the New Testament had been seen in the Old. It was not the message of miracles, signs, or wonders that was too good to be contained; it was the message of peace between God and man.

All my life I saw the Christmas banners that proclaimed, "Peace on earth and goodwill toward men." Those words were always placed in a setting of men having peace and goodwill for one another. Although that is a noble admonition, it is not the true message that was being sent to earth.

For the first time, there would be peace between man and God. Because of the arrival of the Savior, something was going to happen that would make peace between God and man possible. There was going to be a reconciliation. Man was going to be restored to God.

God always wanted peace between Him and man. He put man here in a garden called Paradise. There was perfect harmony between God and man. When man sinned, he did more than disobey God; he acquired a new capability: the ability to determine good and evil for himself. Along with that ability came a self-imposed standard of righteousness and unrighteousness. Through that self-imposed standard, man became fearful of God. He stopped trusting in God's standards of truth and began to develop his own standards. When he failed to meet up to his self-imposed standards, there was self-imposed fear. Man assumed that fear to be from God, and he related to God accordingly. Thus, there was no peace between God and man. This terrible syndrome has continued in the hearts of men until this very day.

With the arrival of the Savior, that fear problem would be resolved; and for the first time since the Garden, there would be peace between God and man. This fear problem was so powerful that man could not be delivered from sin unless he was delivered from fear. Hebrews 2:15 says that Jesus delivered us from the power of evil by delivering us from the fear of death: *"And deliver them who through fear of death were all their lifetime subject to bondage."*

After man sinned, God still wanted man to have the very best, so He gave him the law. The law was not given to make man righteous; there has never been a law that could make man righteous. Rather, the law was given by a loving Father so that man would have a way to avoid falling under the curse of sin. Likewise, it was given so that a sinful, undeserving man could receive the blessing of God. Even when we were dead in sin and enemies of God, He loved us so much that He wanted us to experience the best.

Righteousness demands that sin be paid for in the flesh of the one who commits the sin. Under the law, at best, man could divert the curses. Yet there was never peace under the law. Man was always fearful of judgment. Man was always struggling to measure up. Because man's nature was sinful, there was always the consciousness of sin. There was always fear. There was always enmity between God and man.

Under the law, man feared and therefore did not trust God. All the imaginations of his heart were continually wicked. Thus, under the law, God was angry. As it says in Psalm 7:11, *"God is angry with the wicked every day."* When sin reigned, God was angry. God was required by righteousness to judge sin in the flesh of man.

With the coming of the Messiah, there would be a new day for man and God. Keep in mind that God's plan for man had not changed. God did not change from the old covenant to the new. He had worked every day for four thousand years to bring man into a place to experience His love. But now, through Jesus, it would happen. Finally, a loving relationship between God and man would be possible. There would be peace.

Today, Christians can have what no generation prior to the cross ever had. We can have peace with God. He has dealt with sin. He has made us righteous. He finds no fault with us because we have been washed clean by the blood of the Lamb.

In this environment of peace and acceptance, we can come to God without fear. We can establish a real relationship with Him. We have no need to be afraid that He will reject or hurt us. We are at peace.

Six

જી

# The Chastisement for "Our Peace"

# Six

## ❧

# The Chastisement for "Our Peace"

Once a man is delivered from unrighteousness, he can have peace with God. Because he has peace, he can have fellowship. Fellowship can happen only when enmity is resolved.

*"Therefore being justified by faith, we have peace with God through our Lord Jesus Christ"* (Romans 5:1). The word *"justified"* has the same root as *righteous*. It could read, "Therefore, being made righteous by faith, we have peace with God." If one knows he is righteous, he will be at peace with God. More importantly, God will be at peace with him. And the person will no longer live in fear of judgment and death.

Isaiah 53:5 says, *"But he was wounded for our transgressions, he was bruised for our iniquities: the chastisement of our peace was upon him; and with his stripes* [bruising] *we are healed."* Jesus did not suffer for His sin; He never sinned. He suffered for our transgressions and iniquities. Was this a mere show or type? No. He died for mankind, but He was more than a "sin offering."

For thousands of years, the Jews had gone to the priests and presented an offering that was symbolic of Jesus. Their offering was a type, a shadow; it had no real power to cleanse. Jesus was the real thing. His death was not symbolic; it was the fulfillment of the shadow.

For years, the Jews had stood over their offerings and confessed their sins. Then they would witness and participate in the killing of the sin offering. With their own eyes, they would see this innocent animal receive the death of which they were worthy. Next, they would watch this animal undergo mutilation and burning as payment and appeasement for their sin. They exercised their faith and believed that God would turn His judgment from them because judgment was satisfied in the death of the animal. The blood of the animal did not bring forgiveness, but it did turn away, or appease, God's wrath. Thus the blood signified the judgment of the sin. The sentence of death was passed upon this animal that died as a substitute for the sinner. *"And without shedding of blood is no remission"* (Hebrews 9:22).

An important part of presenting a sacrifice in the old covenant was confessing sins over the offering. Matthew Henry said, "They had to be very specific in their confession, and it had to be done in faith, or God would not receive it." There was never any doubt about this animal being judged for the sins of another. All of this was a symbol of the actual event that would one day take place in the Lord Jesus. While this was the type, the real thing happened at the cross.

At the cross, God made peace with man through a new covenant. This covenant was not secured by the blood of an animal, but by the sinless blood of the Lord Jesus Christ. This covenant was established in His blood. But what does that really mean? In 2 Corinthians 5:21 the Bible says, *"For he hath made him to be sin for us, who knew no sin"; "Him who knew no sin he made to be sin on our behalf"* (ASV); *"For God caused Christ...actually to be sin"* (PHILLIPS). Jesus literally became sin! He was not a mere offering. He literally became sin.

Isaiah 53:6 says it this way: *"And the LORD hath laid on him the iniquity of us all."* In the old covenant, sinful men confessed their sins over their substitute. In this new covenant, a loving God confessed the sins of the world over Jesus. Yet, unlike any other sacrifice, the sins of the world actually came upon Jesus. He became sin.

At this, we begin to understand why Jesus had to become a man. A man brought sin into the world; only a man could bring righteousness into the world. A man brought death; only a man could establish freedom from death. Man sinned, so man had to die. In Jesus the sins of all men were met, and in Him they all were judged.

Prior to the cross, Jesus declared, *"Now is the judgment of this world"* (John 12:31). The judgment of the world for sins took place two thousand years ago. In the King James Version, verse 32 continues to say, *"If I be lifted up...[I] will draw all men unto me."* The word *men* is in italics, which means it is not in the original language. The context of the verse is judgment. Jesus is speaking of the judgment for all men's sin.

When the translators inserted the word *"men"* into this verse, it made it sound like He was saying that all men would be drawn unto Him. This misunderstanding has been a source of many erroneous doctrines. There are people who believe that in the end all men will be saved. It is called the doctrine of ultimate reconciliation. Sadly, not all men will believe and receive Jesus as Lord.

When you remove the word *"men"* from this passage, it reads like this: "Now is the judgment of this world; now the ruler of this world will be cast out. And I, if I am lifted up from the earth, will draw all to Myself." The unanswered question is what will He draw to Himself? The context is judgment. When Jesus died on the cross, He drew the judgment that all men would deserve to Himself. He paid the price that we could not pay.

Until this time, the world (mankind) was an enemy of God. Our sinful nature kept us bound to sin, and then our conscience made us run from God. Similarly, God was obligated to judge sin in man. However, that situation was changed in Jesus.

First John 2:2 says of Jesus, *"And he is the propitiation for our sins."* The word *"propitiation"* has several meanings, but it is best understood as appeasement. Jesus is the appeasement for our sins. To appease something means to satisfy. What was it that Jesus appeased? He appeased the wrath of God, which is the righteous penalty of the law. God's wrath has been satisfied in Jesus. *"Being now justified by his blood, we shall be saved from wrath through Him"* (Romans 5:9). In Jesus, we are made righteous (justified). In Him, the wrath of God is satisfied. How did He do that? He suffered the wrath that we deserve.

*"But God commendeth his love toward us, in that, while we were yet sinners, Christ died for us"* (v. 8). The death of Christ shows God's love for man only when we truly understand the price He paid. Envision this: You have two children. One is always obedient. He always does what you ask and more. The other one is always in trouble. The good child represents Jesus, who is completely obedient and completely satisfying to the Father. The other child represents mankind, who has strayed for 6,000 years.

Imagine these are your children. You leave them at home with specific responsibilities. The dependable one does everything that you asked. The undependable child fails to complete his chores. What's worse is that he breaks one of your most prized possessions.

When you arrive home, you are immediately faced with the uncompleted chores. Then you find your valuable vase broken beyond repair. Your disappointment and anger boils to overflowing. You call both children into the room and begin to question them both very carefully. You discover which child has failed to do his work, and to your amazement, even carelessly broke your valuable vase.

It seems that the issue of punishment would be simple. However, there is a problem. The one you do not want to punish is the one who deserves it. You know he is too frail. He has problems in his life that make him unable to bear the pain of his consequences. Your incredible passion and mercy for this child prevents you from giving him what he deserves. Yet there is still an issue of punishment. At this point the faithful, innocent child says, "Let me pay for the vase." So you lay all the responsibility on him.

This is exactly what God did in Jesus. He knew that mankind, the guilty party, could not pay the price. He created man to be loved, not to be punished. So He allowed Jesus, the innocent Son to pay the full price for our transgressions.

Once the price is paid, wrath and anger are appeased. First John 2:2 says, *"And He Himself is the propitiation for our sins, and not for ours only but also for the whole world"* (NKJV). The word *"propitiation"* means "the satisfying of wrath." Just as the parent's wrath was satisfied when the innocent child paid for the vase, God's wrath was satisfied when Jesus paid the price for our sin. The guilty one doesn't pay, yet the judgment is satisfied.

This is an extreme simplification of the price Jesus paid for man. However, the difference is this: Jesus did not just take the punishment; He literally became the sin. If He had not become sin, man would not be free from the power of sin. Jesus *became* every kind of sin known to man. It was not just the becoming of sin in general; it was the becoming of *our* sins. He took on every sin man would ever commit so that we might be redeemed. He took on the sin of homosexuality. He took on the sin of alcoholism. He was punished as a thief. He was punished a liar. He took on all the sin that the world has. Had He not specifically become our sins, He would not have received our punishment. Remember, even in the Old Testament type, there had to be a specific confession of sins committed. Jesus became your specific sin, and He took your specific penalty. That is why He is worthy to be your Lord.

Because the price has been paid for your specific sins, you have no reason to fear the judgment of God. You have no reason to fear rejection. The chastisement for you to have peace with God was fulfilled in the Lord Jesus. Faith believes this and enters into fellowship with the Father.

We need have no fear of the wrathful chastening of the Lord. Remember, 1 John 4:18 says,

> *His perfect love for us eliminates all dread of what he might do to us. If we are afraid, it is for fear of what he might do to us, and shows that we are not fully convinced that he really loves us.* (TLB)

If we are expecting God to chasten us when we fail, it means that we do not believe in His quality of love and that we reject the sacrifice of Jesus on the cross.

Immediately one looks to Hebrews 12:6: *"For whom the Lord loveth he chasteneth."* There it is: If God loves us, He will chasten us. This is true, but there is a difference in the word *chasten* used in Isaiah and the word used in Hebrews.

The word used in Hebrews is not a word that means to beat or whip. It is a word that is used of training, teaching, and compelling a child to go in the right direction. Yet, if you look up this word *chasten* in many word study books, you will find it as a strong, negative word.

When Catholicism led the church into the Dark Ages, there was much perversion of truth. As a matter of fact, it was the perversion of truth that brought about the Dark Ages, just as it is our perversion of truth that leads us into darkness. During this time, the "church fathers" redefined the meaning of words. They twisted Scripture to provide a means for manipulating and controlling the people.

Archbishop Trench, in his book *Synonyms of the Greek New Testament,* explains how Augustine and other church fathers redefined the meanings of certain words, such as *chastisement* and *discipline,* to have negative connotations.

In their original use, these words were actually very positive. In order to protect their corrupt theology, Augustine acknowledged that these words originally meant to train a child; but in a religious context, he said, they had to give them a stronger meaning. From then until now, we have falsely translated the New Testament word for chastisement.

We have continued to see God as angry. We have refused to go to the cross to interpret our theology. Consequently, we have totally rejected the reality that at the cross Jesus was chastened to deliver us from chastisement.

Let's accept the reality, and with no longer any fear of an angry God chastening us in wrath, we can have peace in our hearts. We can accept peace between us and God.

Seven

જી

# Free from the Penalty

# Seven

### ❧

# Free from the Penalty

*E*veryone knows that God judges sin. Everyone knows that God hates sin. But few realize how God is able to judge sin without destroying man.

You see, while on the cross, Jesus became our sin. At that point, God judged that sin and gave it all the curse it rightfully deserved. Isaiah 53:5 says, *"He was wounded* [tormented] *for our transgressions, he was bruised for our iniquities: the chastisement of our peace was upon him."* When Jesus became sin, God judged sin in Him to deliver us from that judgment.

This is more than deliverance from a future hell. This is deliverance from the curse or the penalty of our sins in this present life. The Jews had a hope of the resurrection, but they did not have any good news about the here and now. They saw God as judgmental and angry until Jesus came and told them the good news about the curse of the law, the good news about God's dealings with sin, the good news that they were free from that penalty *now!*

Galatians 3:13 says it this way: *"Christ hath redeemed us from the curse of the law, being made a curse for us."* Jesus was made a curse for us. In other words, He suffered the curse so that we would not be required to. He redeemed us from the curse of our sin. While Jesus was on that cross, the wrath of God was poured on Him in the form of the curse of the law. All the punishment that we deserve for our sin was suffered by the Lord Jesus. What appreciation we should have! What an awesome price He paid! What a liberty we have! What perfect love God has shown for men!

Unfortunately, most men will never know this wonderful love of God. They will never know to what extremes God went to secure their freedom because the church is preaching an angry God. However, God is no longer angry. His anger has been appeased.

Psalm 22 is one of many psalms that vividly describe the punishment of Jesus while on the cross. It does not take much to grasp that this was more than a sacrifice for sin. This was a sacrifice that became sin and reaped the judgment. The psalm reads,

> *I am poured out like water, and all my bones are out of joint: my heart is like wax; it is melted in the midst of my bowels. My strength is dried up like a potsherd; and my tongue cleaveth to my jaws; and thou hast brought me into the dust of death.* (Psalm 22:14–15)

Why were Jesus' bones out of joint? Why was His torment so much more than the two thieves crucified with Him? Why did His death come so rapidly? According to the Scriptures, Jesus died of something other than mere crucifixion.

Death by crucifixion was slow and painful. It often took days. This is why the soldiers were going to break the legs of the two men who were crucified with Him. The length of time it took to die was a great part of the bitterness of this type of death. Yet, to their amazement, Jesus was already dead at the end of the first day.

Jesus died from the wrath of God as the curse of the law was poured upon Him. Isaiah 53:3 says, *"He is...a man of sorrows, and acquainted with grief."* The words *"sorrows"* and *"grief"* mean sickness and infirmity. Verse 4 goes on to say, *"Surely he hath borne our* [sickness], *and carried our* [infirmities]." This is the way Jesus quoted this verse in Matthew 8:17. Jesus carried our sicknesses and infirmities because they were the results of our sin. They were the curse we deserved.

Under the law, God was obligated to smite the violator with the curse as described in Deuteronomy 28. A major part of that curse was sickness. However, much of it was poverty, torments, and trials. The only way Jesus could set us free from the results of sin was to suffer those results in our place. Otherwise, the righteous requirements of the law would not be satisfied.

After God placed our sin on Jesus, He smote Jesus with the curse. Isaiah 53:5 says, *"And with his stripes we are healed."* For years I was taught that this meant the stripes of the Roman soldiers. For many reasons I could never reconcile that in my heart. Upon closer examination, I found that the word for *"stripes,"* here and in the New Testament, is actually the word *bruised.* Strong's says that the word *chabbuwrah* means "blueness, bruise, hurt, stripe, wound." In other words, "by His bruising we are healed." This is more than just the marks from the soldier's lashings. Verse 5 says, *"He was bruised for our iniquities."* Verse 10 says it pleased God to bruise Him and bring Him to sickness. God bruised Jesus with my sickness. If this is the case, and it is, then I need never fear God bruising me with sickness because Jesus already took it for me.

This is the same thing spoken of in 2 Corinthian 8:9: *"For ye know the grace of our Lord Jesus Christ, that, though he was rich, yet for your sakes he became poor, that ye through his poverty might be rich."* Although Jesus was rich, He had to suffer poverty as a part of the curse of the law. The poverty He suffered was the poverty we were supposed to suffer. Likewise, He was rejected by God so that we would not be rejected. More than that, because of His rejection we always have a guarantee of acceptance.

Jesus suffered every penalty sin would ever deserve. When these things come on us, they are not from God. For God to pour any part of the curse of the law on us would be a denial of the cross of Christ.

The book of Isaiah says that troubles and afflictions will come, but they will not be from God (Isaiah 54:15). You must remember, the devil is a lawbreaker. He does not obey the law of God. He will bring these things on you if you let him.

God has already done His part by setting you free from the curse. You must do your part in resisting the devil. He flees only if you resist him (James 4:7). The resisting is up to you.

First Peter 5:9 says, *"Whom resist stedfast in the faith."* The way to resist the devil is by believing the truth. When we exercise faith—trust in God—we are resisting the devil. He tries to lead us into deceit. If I believe a lie, I cannot benefit from the provisions of God.

I must resist fear; I must resist sickness; I must resist any part of the curse by believing the truth. I am delivered from the penalties that I deserve. I am given the blessings that I do not deserve, because of Jesus and His work on the cross.

The devil's main tools against humanity are deceit and ignorance. If we are ignorant of the things of the cross, we will think God is tormenting us for our failure. Although we may deserve it, it is never God who torments.

In this life, man often finds himself yielding to sin. Nevertheless, because we have been freed from the penalty of sin, we do not lose our relationship with God when we sin. Because we are free from the penalty, we are free from the fear that could separate us from the only source of help.

When there is a penalty, man is compelled to defend himself. This leads to lying, deceit, and all manner of sin. When there is no penalty, the pure of heart are free to receive help from a loving God.

# Eight

&

# The Exchange

# Eight

## ℬ

# The Exchange

*For when we were yet without strength, in due time Christ
died for the ungodly....But God commendeth his love toward
us, in that, while we were yet sinners, Christ died for us. Much
more then, being now justified by his blood, we shall be saved
from wrath through him. For if, when **we were enemies,** we
were reconciled to God by the death of his Son, much more,
being reconciled, we shall be saved by his life. And not only so,
but we also joy [boast] in God through our Lord Jesus Christ,
by whom we have now received the atonement.*
—Romans 5:6, 8–11, emphasis added

*T*he Bible is clear about the fact that we were once
enemies of God. Colossians 1:21 explains this very
clearly: *"And you, that were sometime alienated and
enemies in your mind by wicked works, yet now hath he reconciled."* God has never been our enemy, but we have been
enemies of God.

Colossians says we were enemies in our minds by wicked
works. In other words, that status existed only in our minds.
It was not real. It was all in our heads, so to speak. God has

never been the enemy of mankind. God has always worked to restore and deliver mankind from sin and its effects.

Yet, when we sin, our hearts condemn us. We become afraid of God. We actually judge Him and determine that He must hate us for our wickedness. We assume how He must feel about the situation, and we act accordingly.

God solved this problem by making peace with us through the cross. Colossians 1:20 says, *"And, having made peace through the blood of his cross, by him to reconcile all things unto himself; by him, I say, whether they be things in earth, or things in heaven."*

When God solved this problem, He poured the curse of the law upon Jesus, delivering us from the penalty of our sin. God did not, however, stop at merely delivering us from wrath. His ultimate goal was to cause us to experience His love, life, and acceptance whereby we would enter into a meaningful relationship with Him.

Galatians clearly points out that God not only freed us from the curse, but He also put us in a position to receive all the promises and blessings that He made in times past. *"Christ hath redeemed us from the curse of the law...that the blessing of Abraham might come...that we might receive the promise of the Spirit"* (Galatians 3:13–14).

Freedom from wrath is only half the work of the cross. The word *reconciled* has several very strong and positive meanings. One is exchange. When we were enemies of God, we were exchanged to God. Beyond dying for our sins, Jesus took our place in order that we might take His place. In other words, He received what we were and what our lives deserved, while we receive what He is and what His life deserves.

In John 10:10 Jesus said it this way: *"I am come that they might have life, and that they might have it more abundantly."* He did not come just to set us free from the results of our sin. He also came to put us in the center of God's will so that we might receive God's blessings and promises.

God has always desired that man have His best. That was clearly demonstrated in the Garden of Eden. Adam was placed there in abundance and provision. There was no lack, suffering, or sickness, and there was no pain in the Garden of Eden. God proved His desire for man with the utopian setting He created for man. It was man, not God, who surrendered Paradise to make it the world it is today. Destruction, pain, suffering, sickness, and poverty all came in with sin. Sin was introduced by the devil and brought into Paradise by man. This was not God's desire or His judgment. It was the law of sowing and reaping.

Throughout Bible history, you see God's desire to pour His blessings on men. When God found men and women who believed Him and obeyed Him, He showered them with His goodness. Many of the patriarchs were very wealthy men. Some of them would even be multimillionaires by today's standards. Even the law gave provision for God's blessings. He has always wanted us to live in His provision and power. The stipulations of the law gave opportunity for curses, but it also gave the same opportunity for the blessings or promises. The law was filled with wonderful promises from God. These promises included health, healing, prosperity, success, peace, and joy. But you had to live a holy life before God to qualify for those blessings.

The weakness of the law was the flesh (Romans 8:3). Because the flesh was weak, man continually found himself in a position worthy of the curses. And because the flesh was weak, man seldom found himself in a position to receive the blessings. The entire law was based on the performance of man. The new covenant, on the other hand, is based on the performance of one Man, Christ Jesus.

Jesus was the One who lived the sinless life. He also was the One who became sin, suffered the penalty for sin, and then conquered sin by the Resurrection. The entire new covenant depends on the completed work of the Lord Jesus. We participate in that accomplished work by faith.

Romans 5:11 in the King James Version says that in Jesus we have *now* received atonement. The word *atonement* is almost the same as the word *reconciled* in the previous verses, and it means the same thing. In other words, in Jesus we have the exchange, and it is effective now. The exchange will not go into effect in some future time or dispensation; it went into effect when Jesus sat down at the right hand of the Father. We begin to participate in it the moment we believe it.

The word *atonement* as used in the old covenant is not found anywhere in the new covenant. Atonement means "covering" in the Hebrew language. The only thing the Old Testament believers received from the blood of the animals was a covering.

You do not have a covering in Jesus; you have an exchange—an exchange that took your sin away from you and gave you His righteousness. Your sins are not covered; they no longer exist. God is not pretending that they do not exist. *They do not exist.* When He looks at you, He does not pretend that you are righteous. You are righteous by the Lord Jesus.

When Jesus was raised from the dead, He conquered sin and death. He did not conquer sin in general; He conquered your specific sin, thereby guaranteeing you a specific victory over your specific sin. He was raised up in newness of life. The quality of life that Jesus now has is the quality of life the Father has. In Him, you receive that quality of life as well.

The Greek word used to describe the quality of life we have in Jesus is *zoe.* This is a quality of life that is possessed by the one who gives it. Because Jesus received this quality of life from the Father, I receive it, too. Remember, the inheritance He earned is the one I receive. I have the quality of life God has. I received it in the Lord Jesus.

In the exchange, we receive His righteousness. That righteousness qualifies us to receive all the promises of God. Colossians 1:12 says, *"Giving thanks unto the Father, which hath made us meet to be partakers of the inheritance of the saints in light." The New International Version* translates the word *"meet"* as *"qualified."* In other words, God has qualified us to receive the inheritance. How did He qualify us? In Jesus.

I receive nothing from God on my own merit. Instead, I receive every promise based on the finished work of Jesus. Thus the Scripture is fulfilled that says, *"No flesh should glory* [boast] *in his presence"* (1 Corinthians 1:29). My confidence is not in my accomplishments but in Jesus' accomplishments. I am qualified by Him, and I receive that inheritance by faith— not faith that says I am able, not faith that says I am worthy, not even faith that says I have enough faith, but faith that says Jesus did it all.

Because I am in Jesus and have His righteousness, every promise God ever made to anyone in the Bible is mine. *"For all the promises of God in him are yea, and in him Amen, unto the glory of God"* (2 Corinthians 1:20). Because I am free from works-righteousness, I can rest in Jesus with no fear or dread. Furthermore, I am compelled to a life of worship and praise.

I cannot help but continually give thanks to the One who has done so much for me. Because I know I am righteous, my heart desires righteousness; because I know I am free from sin, I am confidently compelled to stay free from sin. Why should I sin? I am righteous in Jesus.

On this issue, we are very prone to mix the old covenant with the new one. We are very quick to return to works as our basis of receiving from God. But if we are in works, then it is no more a promise. *"Now to him that worketh is the reward not reckoned of grace, but of debt"* (Romans 4:4). Works say that God owes. Grace and faith say that God promised.

Works say that I can get God to respond to me. Faith (trust) is my response to what God has done in Jesus. Works place the emphasis on what I have done. Faith places the emphasis on what Jesus has done. Works look to my righteousness for qualification. Faith looks to Jesus' righteousness for qualification.

The life I now live is the exchanged life. Jesus received what I deserve; I receive what He deserves. He was made to be my sin; I was made to be His righteousness. He received the penalties that my sin deserved; I am receiving the blessings that His righteousness deserves. Because He was rejected, I am accepted. Because He was chastened, I have peace before God. By Him I have been exchanged to God.

# Nine

&

# Faith-Righteousness

# Nine

## ∞

# Faith-Righteousness

*P*aul, as an apostle to the Gentiles, was given special insight into our identity in Jesus. Why? He was dealing with people who had no knowledge of the law, and God did not want them under law. He did not want them to try to mix law and grace. Therefore, He sent them a man who had lived by the letter of the law, yet still needed Jesus.

Paul, more than anyone, knew the futility of works-righteousness. Repeatedly, he spoke of who we are in Christ. All we have and all we do would be the result of the finished work of the Lord Jesus. Remember, he was sent to people who had no hope in the law. When the Judaizers came and tried to mix law with faith, he continually confirmed that Christ in us was the *"hope of glory"* (Colossians 1:27). We need not hope in the law.

We need not trust in any of our good works. But we must find our assurance in Christ Jesus, our one and only hope of glory. Paul knew that the secret of God's power was faith-righteousness, a message that still confuses the carnally minded.

Faith-righteousness is a message that is understood only by revelation, yet it is a message that is essential to every believer's victory. Without the absolute confidence of right standing before God, there cannot be an absolute assurance of the promises. And it is by these promises that we escape the corruption that is in the world through lust (2 Peter 1:4).

Paul knew that works-righteousness did not bring freedom, but bondage. It actually produced bondage! He also knew that faith-righteousness was the only way to know Jesus. It is the only way to fellowship or share in what was accomplished in His sufferings. And it is the only way to know the power of His resurrection (Philippians 3:10). People who never enter into faith-righteousness never get real freedom from the flesh and the various sins that work in the flesh.

Paul discounted all his works, all his qualifications, and all his personal accomplishments so that he might *"be found in him, not having mine own righteousness, which is of the law, but that which is through the faith of Christ, the righteousness which is of God by faith"* (Philippians 3:9). Faith-righteousness places Jesus at the very center of all we are, all we have, and all we can do in God. It acknowledges the vanity of our own attempts at righteousness and depends on Jesus' righteousness to be manifest in every area of life.

Faith-righteousness is the heart of the message of the cross, because on that cross an exchange took place. In that exchange, God *"made him to be sin for us, who knew no sin; that we might be made the righteousness of God in him"* (2 Corinthians 5:21). It is this message of the cross that will liberate us from sin and deliver us from the works of the flesh.

If we do not believe in righteousness by exchange, there is nothing left but works-righteousness. By the works of the law or flesh, no man has ever been justified (Galatians 2:16). Works-righteousness is a life of legalism that leaves out the grace of God, which works in us to deliver us from sin. It places man and his performance at the center.

In Richard Lenski's commentary on Romans, he talks about the realm of law and the realm of works. The Bible often speaks of law and works. When speaking of law, it is not limited to the old covenant law. It could be any realm of law. Anything we do to earn something from God, anything we do apart from faith, anything we do to make us righteous, is in the realm of law, works, and flesh. It is also sin (Romans 14:23). It is sin because it rejects the work of Jesus.

The term *flesh* is much like the term *law.* When the Bible speaks of the flesh, it is not talking about this body. It is talking about a realm where we are trying to be made righteous by our own abilities. It is the performance-oriented life. People who try to relate to God on the basis of works of law are in the flesh.

It was essential that we be delivered from law in order to be delivered from the flesh. Romans 7:5 says, *"For when we were in the flesh, the motions* [passions] *of sins, which were by the law, did work in our members."* Law or works causes passion to arise in our bodies. Until we are free from works, we cannot conquer sin.

In the exchange, we died to the law by the body of Christ (v. 4). Remember, when Christ died, we died. Now that we are delivered from the law (the realm of law), we are able to serve God in newness of spirit and not in the oldness of the letter.

In other words, we are no longer doing the best we can and hoping that it will be acceptable to God. We are believing that we are righteous because of Jesus and trusting the Spirit of God to change us and empower us to live in righteousness. Being in the Spirit is not when we are in a trancelike, mystical state of mind. It is when we are dependent on the Spirit to empower us for righteousness, thereby delivering us from the realm of the flesh.

When we try to serve God in the oldness of the letter, whether it is the old covenant or the new covenant turned to law, sin will revive. *"For I was alive without the law once: but when the commandment came, sin revived"* (Romans 7:9). Sin comes back to life in a heart that has no room for faith-righteousness. Sin thrives where man tries to operate in his own ability. Even if we are able to conquer a problem by the sheer power of our will, we become self-righteous. One way or another, sin revives.

Romans 6:14 states that the very reason we are free from sin is that we are no longer under law, but under grace. Grace is God's ability working in us. Works and law frustrate the grace of God (Galatians 2:21). The word *frustrate* means "to set aside or nullify, make void, disesteem, and neutralize." When we enter the realm of works, God's power to free us from sin is nullified. Therefore, sin will always dominate the man who lives in the realm of works.

Many people have debated exactly what Romans 7 refers to. Is it Paul before he got saved, or after he got saved? Personally, I believe it describes the plight of any person who departs from faith and grace and enters the realm of works. Likewise, when Paul talked about falling from grace in Galatians 5:4, he was not discussing whether the person would go to heaven. He was discussing leaving the realm of grace (God's ability) and entering back into our own ability.

Christ is of no effect in the life of the person bound to works. We must accept our righteousness in Jesus. This is totally contrary to all the natural aspects of man. We all look at our own failures and shortcomings and say, "How can I call myself righteous? I have all kinds of problems and sins!" Yet we will never be really free from those sins until we receive His righteousness.

Receiving that righteousness starts with believing. If Jesus' mission was accomplished, and it was, then *you are righteous in Christ.* If you believe that, you will not be able to live any kind of life you choose. If you believe it, you will confess it, thank God for it, and live in step with the Spirit of Christ.

The power of righteousness comes alive in the person who believes he is righteous in Jesus. That person has a "righteousness conscience." On the other hand, the person who is operating in law has a consciousness of sin. What we have awareness of grows in our life. Accordingly, the person aware of sin falls into more sin, and the person aware of righteousness grows in a life of righteousness.

After explaining the exchange, Romans 5:12 gives this example: Sin entered the world through one man. Few people have trouble with this. We all know that we are sinners because of Adam. In him, we all became sinners. We were born with a sin nature. Now, before you got saved, I am sure you did some good things, but those good things did not make you righteous. You were still a sinner. It was your nature to sin. Despite your efforts, you always went back to sin—*sin was your nature.* Keep in mind, doing good occasionally did not cause you to have a righteous nature.

Because of the sin of Adam, the sentence of death was passed upon all men. You did nothing to receive the ability to die; you were born with that ability. However, likewise, in Jesus, by His life we receive the gift of righteousness (Romans

5:17). Natural birth guarantees us a sin nature, but a spiritual birth guarantees us a righteous nature by the gift of righteousness. Just as sin passed the judgment of death on all men, righteousness passes the life of God unto all men. You will recall from our discussion in chapter eight that the word for *life* in the original language is the word *zoe*. According to the *Biblio-Theological Lexicon of New Testament Greek, zoe* is the quality of life of the one who gives it. Because we have Jesus' righteousness, we get to participate in the *zoe* life of God. This life makes available to us everything that God has and is. And more importantly, it is a product of Jesus' righteousness.

Romans 5:10 says it this way: *"Being reconciled* [exchanged], *we shall be saved by his life* [*zoe*]." The word *"saved"* means more than born again. It means healed, delivered, protected, made whole, made well, and so on. The reason we have this complete salvation is that we receive His *zoe*. We receive His *zoe* because we receive His righteousness. We receive His righteousness because of the exchange. Accordingly, it is all ours by faith.

You are righteous because you were born of God. Being righteous does not mean you never sin. It means you have a righteous nature. It is now natural for you to live a righteous life. Even though you may fall, you are not a sinner. As the psalmist said, *"Though he fall, he shall not be utterly cast down: for the LORD upholdeth him with his hand"* (Psalm 37:24). Proverbs says it like this: *"For a just man falleth seven times, and riseth up again: but the wicked shall fall into mischief"* (Proverbs 24:16).

When you had a sin nature, you did some good works occasionally. However, those good works could not change your unrighteous nature to become righteous. Likewise, now that you have a righteous nature, when you fall, that cannot change your righteous nature to make you unrighteous. We were born into unrighteousness. Our works did not bring about that state of being. Likewise, we are born into righteousness; our works will not bring about that state of being.

This is not a permit to sin. On the contrary, a righteous heart hates sin. A righteous heart wants to please God. A righteous heart loves righteousness. And the heart is made righteous only by faith (Romans 5:1; 10:10).

There is a fear in us that this belief will somehow make it possible for men to get away with things. And some could try to use it as a license to sin. But Paul, Peter, and John warned against and dealt with these same fears. There were groups in the early church that tried to abuse freedom. The apostles, though, dealt with the issue without abandoning this truth.

To abandon faith-righteousness is to abandon the finished work of Jesus. Regardless of how sincere the motive, a departure from faith-righteousness is a departure from truth.

Ten

&

# Faith to Faith

# Ten

## ଛ

# Faith to Faith

*T*he weakness of modern Christianity traces back to the foundation of our belief system. Everything we believe is slanted in the direction of and interpreted by our foundational beliefs. Our one and only foundation should be the death, burial, and resurrection of the Lord Jesus.

The slight deviations from what happened at the cross are what create confusion and destruction in the major areas of our lives. It's like firing a weapon. When a bullet is fired from a gun, the barrel must be exact. A deviation of only a fraction of an inch could result in a miss of many feet. And the farther the bullet travels from the barrel of the gun, the greater the degree of error.

Likewise, there are many things we believe about the cross that may not really seem significant until we weave them into our daily lives. Then, in that setting, we end up miles away from our desired destination in Christ.

Paul said in Romans 1:16, *"For I am not ashamed of the gospel of Christ: for it is the power of God unto salvation to every one that believeth; to the Jew first, and also to the Greek."*

The Gospel is the *"power of God unto salvation."* It should produce the salvation of God. We know that salvation is more than being born again. It is the full benefit of God's provision. So if what we believe is not producing salvation, then we must face the truth: Either we do not believe the truth, or maybe what we do believe is not true.

When Paul said he was not ashamed of the Gospel, he was not speaking of Jesus personally. The Jews did not have that great of a problem with Jesus. They had a problem with what Jesus had accomplished for man. The Judaizers who followed Paul around the world and caused so much of his persecution did not tell people to reject Jesus. They simply told people that Jesus could not make you righteous.

The good news of Jesus is that righteousness is now a free gift. Any deviation from this is not good news. The Jews had righteousness by works. In Christianity, we have so compromised the Gospel that today we have no more than the Jews had.

In verse 17 Paul continued, *"For therein is the righteousness of God revealed from faith to faith: as it is written, The just shall live by faith."* Paul said that in the Gospel, the righteousness of God is *"revealed from faith to faith."* He did not say that it was revealed from faith to works.

Most Christians actually believe that Jesus saves you, but that your works make you righteous. Jesus gets you saved; you keep yourself saved. Jesus purchased your healing; you qualify yourself to receive healing. Jesus conquered the devil; your works deliver you from his attacks. We do not really believe that righteousness begins with faith and ends with faith.

Faith-righteousness should be woven through every thread of our belief system. The moment we depart from faith-righteousness, we have departed from the Gospel. It must be the basis for all we are, all we hope to be, and all we will receive from God.

The Galatians had this same problem. Paul preached Jesus to them. They received a wonderful salvation. When Paul left, the Judaizers came in and said, "Believe on Jesus for salvation, but you must obey all the law to be righteous enough to receive the promises. If you don't live holy enough, God will smite you with the curses."

This is why Paul said, *"Are ye so foolish? having begun in the Spirit, are ye now made perfect by the flesh?"* (Galatians 3:3). In other words, this work was begun in you by the Spirit of God, and it can be completed only by the Spirit of God.

In Galatians 3:2, 5, Paul asked,

> *This only would I learn of you, Received ye the Spirit by the works of the law, or by the hearing of faith?...He therefore that ministereth to you the Spirit, and worketh miracles among you, doeth he it by the works of the law, or by the hearing of faith?*

In other words, when you first received the Spirit, was it because you believed what you heard or because you earned it by keeping enough of the law? When people worked miracles among you, was it because people believed the truth or because they earned it by keeping the law?

Nothing changes in this regard after we are saved. This relationship with God was the product of a free gift. Our ability to maintain a relationship with God is the product of that free gift. Paul told the Colossian believers to continue in Christ the same way they began in Christ—rooted and grounded in faith. Don't try to change the rules.

Nearly every book of the New Testament was written because the churches were being deceived in the area of righteousness. While believing on the person of Jesus, they rejected His finished work of the cross. They believed they were saved by grace and made righteous by works. They didn't believe righteousness was from faith to faith.

This issue of righteousness is the stumbling block of the Gospel. People do not struggle with most of the major aspects of Jesus' life and ministry. They struggle with this issue of righteousness.

In Romans, Paul described the dilemma:

> *What shall we say then? That the Gentiles, which followed not after righteousness, have attained to righteousness, even the righteousness which is of faith. But Israel, which followed after the law of righteousness, hath not attained to the law of righteousness.*
> (Romans 9:30–31)

Israel really wanted to find righteousness, but they could not find it. The Gentiles were not really looking for righteousness, but they found it.

Verse 32 explains why the Jews were unable to attain righteousness: *"Wherefore? Because they sought it not by faith, but as it were by the works of the law."* The Gentiles were willing to accept righteousness as a gift. That response is faith. The Jews, on the other hand, were not willing to accept that it was a gift. They sought to earn righteousness by their performance.

The last phrase of verse 32 is of the utmost importance: *"For they stumbled at that stumblingstone."* Faith-righteousness is the stumbling block of the Gospel. This is the rock of offense.

Jesus Himself is not the rock of offense. Jesus, as our righteousness, is what offends and causes those who will not believe to stumble. They stumble because of their unbelief concerning righteousness.

Romans 9:33 says, *"As it is written, Behold, I lay in Sion a stumblingstone and rock of offence: and whosoever believeth on him shall not be ashamed."* If a person believes on Jesus as his righteousness, he will not stumble; he will not be ashamed; he will not be confounded. But those who do not believe will stumble.

They rejected the cornerstone. Jesus, as our righteousness, is the Cornerstone of Christianity. Anything else will produce a faulty foundation. When we try to build on another foundation, the entire building will collapse. This is why Paul warned in 1 Corinthians 3:10–11 about the need to take heed when building our lives:

> *According to the grace of God which is given unto me, as a wise masterbuilder, I have laid the foundation, and another buildeth thereon. But let every man take heed how he buildeth thereupon. For other foundation can no man lay than that is laid, which is Jesus Christ.*

We should continue in our Christian life. We should grow in our understanding of God. We should grow in good works. But all these things should be built upon the foundation of faith-righteousness. They should never be the foundation of our righteousness. Every Christian should live a godly life. Every Christian should bear fruit. However, the moment these things become our hope and confidence for being accepted by God, they are no longer gold, silver, and precious stones. Because they are not built on the foundation, they are wood, hay, and stubble.

Healing is true, but if it is not built on the foundation of faith-righteousness, it will collapse. All the promises of God are true, but they will not stand when built on a faulty foundation. We are like people who have tried to build skyscrapers on mud puddles. When the building falls, we question the validity of the promise. The promises are good, but they must be built upon the sure foundation of Jesus as our righteousness. Our every belief must be built upon faith-righteousness. The only righteousness that qualifies us for all the promises is His righteousness.

Eleven

&

# Being Righteous We "Have Peace"

## Eleven

ဢ

# Being Righteous We "Have Peace"

From the giving of the law at Mount Sinai, the Jews had to earn the blessings of God. As we stated earlier, if they were good (righteous), they received the blessings. If they were unrighteous, they received the curses. Keep in mind that it is God who established His standard of righteousness. God is the only One who can define and determine the standards of right and wrong. Any attempt on our part to define righteousness apart from the Word of God is actually humanism. That is exactly what Adam did in the Garden of Eden.

From the time that Adam partook of the fruit of the Tree of Knowledge of Good and Evil, man has been a god unto himself. He has decided right and wrong by his own definition. He even has attempted to make God accept his standards. The ability to determine right and wrong, however, belongs only to God. Keep in mind, that was satan's basic temptation: "You can be gods and determine right and wrong for yourselves." This is where we have the birth of humanism, which is the basis for all false religion.

Humanism places man at the center of the universe. His personal opinions are the determining factors for right and wrong. Man is a god to himself. He makes his own standards and his own rules. But worst of all, he fabricates his own definition of righteousness. This is a right that belongs only to God.

The word *heresy* is used very loosely in Christian circles. Usually, we define a heretic to be anyone who disagrees with our beliefs. The word *heresy,* however, has its roots in a word that means "to choose." So a heretic is one who chooses what he believes. The Word of God is not the absolute authority for a heretic. He views truth as optional; therefore, he lives life by preference instead of conviction.

One becomes a Christian by making Jesus Lord of his life. As Lord, His Word is the final authority about what we should believe. It should form all our views and opinions. Regardless of how we may feel about a particular thing, we surrender the right of choice to His lordship. When one enters the realm of choice about his beliefs, he is functioning outside the realm of Christ's lordship. This option of choice has been a detrimental factor for the church down through the ages. We have chosen to believe many wrong things about God, about the cross of Christ, and about how to have a relationship with God.

Church history reveals that man has continually opted for beliefs that are more convenient or less threatening. For example, baptism by immersion was the standard for hundreds of years. Later, when it was not convenient, the church modified it to sprinkling. This was more socially acceptable.

Some people have a false concept of God as an angry taskmaster. However, we see God's character revealed in Jesus. He said, "If you've seen Me, you've seen the Father." (See John 14:9.) He was the exact representation of God. God would not relate to man in any fashion contrary with Jesus' life and ministry. When Jesus was confronted with the adulteress, He didn't judge her. Yet we insist that God is angry and faultfinding. Why? It is a convenient way to control others.

Christianity is not a religion of choice and convenience. Rather, we come to God hurting and faced with all sorts of problems that are the product of decisions based on our personal beliefs. Our lives cannot change if our beliefs do not change. One cannot come to Jesus and experience any change apart from surrendering his beliefs.

One who does not surrender his views and opinions to God will continue to be a god unto himself. He also will continue to experience the same hurts and difficulties as before. God works in our lives as a product of believing the truth.

The greatest devastation in the Christian's life comes about by the refusal to accept God's standard and definition of righteousness. Because we do not understand faith-righteousness, we cling to works-righteousness. After all, it makes sense; we can understand it. It does not require us to believe something that is beyond our present scope of understanding.

We all understand works-righteousness. It works like this: If I do only good things, I am acceptable to God and I get the blessings. If I do anything wrong, I am unacceptable to God, and I get chastened.

We saw it under the law. It was revived in the early church and ushered into the Dark Ages. Much of the theology that was developed by the early Catholic Church, particularly in this area, still influences our concept of God. Works-righteousness, though, always brings fear and rejection. One never knows if what he has done is good enough. One doesn't have the confidence of God's forgiveness. This fear is torment. The only deliverance from that torment is believing and experiencing the love of God (1 John 4:8).

In Romans 1:16 Paul said, *"I am not ashamed of the gospel* [the Good News] *of Christ: for it* [this Good News] *is the power of God unto salvation* [new birth, healing, deliverance, protection, and so on]." When one does not believe the Good News, he is void of the power of God. He is unable to live the salvation Jesus purchased for us. Whatever part of the Good News you believe, you can receive the power to live.

Paul went on to say in verse 17, *"For therein* [in this Good News] *is the righteousness of God revealed from faith to faith."* Faith-righteousness is the Good News. Faith-righteousness is the beginning and the end of the Christian life. It does not go from faith to works; it is faith to faith. This is why the people of the early church were called believers. Everything they experienced with God was a product of what they believed, not a product of what they did. The old covenant was the product of works. Righteous works qualified you to receive the provision of God. But we have a new and different covenant. It is a better covenant, with better promises.

God has established a new covenant. He intended that we would be free from the old one. He set us free from works-righteousness to qualify us to receive the life (*zoe*) that is earned by Jesus. Yet we stay bound to the old. We cling to works-righteousness simply because we do not believe and understand faith-righteousness. We enter into the realm of choice and justify it by our own reasoning. Sadly, we are the ones who suffer for it. We make the sacrifice of Jesus void of power through our traditional beliefs (Mark 7:13).

Works-righteousness appeals to the carnal mind. The carnal mind, according to Romans 8:5, is a mind set on the flesh. Remember, we live in the flesh when we attempt to be made righteous by the works of the flesh. To the carnal mind, works-righteousness makes sense. It is rational. It fits our preferential beliefs.

Romans 8:5 says, *"For they that are after the flesh do mind the things of the flesh; but they that are after the Spirit the things of the Spirit."* The person whose mind is set on what the flesh does is a person who has man and his works at the center of his religion. He erroneously places God on the outside. This mind is not set on the work of the Spirit of Christ. It has no awareness or sensitivity to the reality that righteousness is a work of the Spirit of righteousness.

Thus, Romans 8:8 declares, *"So then they that are in the flesh cannot please God."* Why? you ask. Hebrews 11:6 says it this way: *"But without faith it is impossible to please him."* Galatians 2:16 says it another way:

> Knowing that a man is not justified by the works of the law, but by the faith of Jesus Christ, even we have believed in Jesus Christ, that we might be justified by the faith of Christ, and not by the works of the law: for by the works of the law shall no flesh be justified.

God has defined righteousness. We cannot reject His definition for our reasonable, rational preferences.

The great restraint concerning faith-righteousness is that we do not *understand* it. We have mistakenly thought that we could believe by understanding. There is some truth to that in the natural realm, but the Bible presents just the opposite. In the spiritual realm, we must believe in order to understand. Hebrews 11:3 explains, *"Through faith we understand."* As we choose to believe God, understanding is opened to us. Therefore, we will never understand what we do not believe.

Why is it so essential that we receive righteousness as a gift? All of this may seem trivial until we see the practical difference it will make. Romans 5:1 says, *"Therefore being justified* [made righteous] *by faith, we have peace with God through our Lord Jesus Christ."* God is at peace with man. We have established that. But why is it so important that we see that?

Although God is at peace with us, we might not be at peace with Him. If we are living in fear or insecurity about our relationship with God, we cannot break free from sin. We have already seen how a works mentality actually causes sin to resurrect in our members. Law causes us to hide our sin. Mercy and forgiveness, on the other hand, create an environment of peace and love that lets us deal with our sin.

Until we can deal openly with our sin before God, we cannot be set free from it. We cannot deal openly and honestly with it if we do not realize God's peace. An environment that says God will judge you for your sin is a negative, unproductive environment. It is one that promotes self-righteousness and deceit. We become defensive of our actions. Instead of being teachable, we are ready to defend our every position. After all, if we are wrong, we run the risk of judgment. Yet if God poured all His judgment out on Jesus, we need not fear that He will judge us.

Many ministers are afraid of this message. They fear it will promote a loose and casual lifestyle. They are afraid people will take advantage of God's goodness and get into sin. Actually, if people believe this, they will be less compelled to sin. When one believes in the *"zoe"* life of God, when he sees all the good things God has to offer, when he sees the goodness of God, he will also see that the world has nothing to offer.

Most people believe the world has good things to offer in comparison to the false "suffering message" of Christianity.

They think that being a Christian is a defeated lifestyle of eating crumbs and wearing worn-out clothes. That is simply not true. Try to explain that to Abraham, David, and the other patriarchs!

There is indeed a time of scriptural suffering, but we should not suffer because of unbelief or ignorance. If I must suffer for the Gospel, I will do it gladly. Even in that suffering, I am victorious. Or, if I must suffer, I will suffer as Jesus did. Hebrews 2:18 says He suffered when He was tempted. His suffering was in denying Himself, living for God, and saying no to sin. I will gladly say no to sin and self. This is what it means to take up my cross. I also will suffer by surrendering my will, my opinions, and my preferences to His will, His view, and His opinion.

The message of wrath, suffering, trials, and testing has turned the world away from the Gospel. As a matter of fact, this is not the Gospel (Good News) at all. The world will be won by the Good News. The news that God is not angry with you; the news that God loves you; the news that righteousness is a free gift; the news that your sins have been paid for; the news that Jesus provided all of this is the Good News the world needs to hear. The message of wrath does not keep people from sin; it makes them hypocrites and liars. They do not stay out of sin any better than anyone else; they just hide it better. A person who wants to sin will sin, regardless of what he believes. Whatever his theological position, he will find a way to justify his sin. Before a person can properly deal with sin, he must be free from the fear of judgment.

God said, *"Come...let us reason together"* (Isaiah 1:18). There is no reasoning with wrath. In fact, the book of Proverbs warns against dealing with angry, unreasonable people. Our reasoning with God is not trying to convince Him we are right or justified in our sin. Our reasoning with God is where we come face-to-face with a loving God in an environment of peace and confess our sins. It is here that mercy and truth meet together. It is here that the goodness of God draws us into repentance (Romans 2:4). It is here that a troubled and convicted heart finds mercy and grace to help in time of need (Hebrews 4:16).

If I am not fully convinced that I am righteous through the Lord Jesus, I will never have peace. I will never be sure. Recently I sat and talked with a person who had gone into error. This person believed that everyone would eventually go to heaven. As we discussed why she believed this she said, "I used to be so afraid that I might not be forgiven and that I might go to hell. When I heard this, it gave me peace." The absence of peace makes people susceptible to error that offers false peace.

Many people have given up on God and returned to sin. When I talked to one man he said, "I just could not go on not knowing if God had really forgiven me." Because he did not know he was righteous, he did not have peace. That lack of peace destroyed his walk with God.

Then there are those who are bitter. They have labored to do right. They attempted to earn the blessings. When they did not get peace or when they did not get the reward they expected, they became bitter and angry at God.

Our peace cannot be based on our performance; that is too unpredictable. It causes us to vacillate up and down. Neither can our peace be in a false doctrine. Then we would have to defend that doctrine to maintain our peace. Our peace must be rooted in the certainty of the finished work of Jesus.

If Jesus is my righteousness, He is the center of my life. For every promise in the Bible, I look to Him and His finished work and say, "Because of You, I am qualified." When trouble comes my way, I look to Jesus and say, "Because of You, I know this is not from God." When fear tries to enter my mind, I look to Jesus and say, "Because of You, I don't have to be afraid. *You are my peace.*"

# Twelve

&

# The Covenant of Peace

# Twelve

## ෨

# The Covenant of Peace

*I*saiah 53 graphically describes the exchange that took place on the cross. It depicts the terrible suffering that Jesus endured for our sakes. Then, chapter 54 begins to explain the new covenant that will go into effect as a result of that exchange.

Isaiah 54:7–8 says,

> *For a small moment have I forsaken thee; but with great mercies will I gather thee. In a little wrath I hid my face from thee for a moment; but with everlasting kindness will I have mercy on thee, saith the LORD thy Redeemer.*

Before God could have fellowship with man, He had to settle the sin problem. Sin had to be judged. Righteousness demands the judgment of sin.

God, in His great love for man, judged the sin of the world in Jesus. Because His wrath and righteous judgment have already taken place, man is now free to enter into a peaceful relationship with a holy God. Before His wrath was appeased, the consequence of sin was the main thing that kept men walking upright.

The fear of penalty may change one's actions, but it will not change one's heart. The heart is changed by love. Since God is a heart God (1 Samuel 16:7), He desires a relationship. Now that judgment has been satisfied, God can love us into a heart relationship.

Romans 2:4 says it is *"the goodness of God* [that] *leadeth …to repentance."* The word *"repentance,"* contrary to popular teaching, is not a grieving or weeping. It may include those elements, but that is not repentance. In fact, the Bible talks about two kinds of repentance. One is an afterthought because of consequences. This is what the Bible speaks of when it says that Judas repented before committing suicide (Matthew 27:3).

The repentance that God requires is a change of mind. Judas did not change his mind about his sin; he simply was sorry for the results. The judgment message may make one dread the results, but it will not change the heart. If we have a loving relationship with a loving God, that relationship will draw us into a change of mind. It will bring us to the place where we do not desire to sin.

I so enjoy and depend on my loving, heavenly Father that I do not want to sin. His goodness is too precious to me to disrupt it with sin. This is not to say I never sin, but this is the motivation for staying out of sin. Likewise, this is the motivation for repentance.

Isaiah 54:9 goes on to say,

> *For this is as the waters of Noah unto me: for as I have sworn that the waters of Noah should no more go over the earth; so have I sworn that I would not be wroth with thee, nor rebuke thee.*

In His covenant with Noah, God swore that He would never judge the earth by water again. He then set the rainbow in the sky as a seal to that covenant. God has faithfully kept that promise.

Now He says, "This is just like My covenant with Noah." In other words, this covenant is just as sure as His covenant with Noah. This covenant says, "I will never be angry with you or rebuke you" (Isaiah 54:9). This is what God has sworn to us, and this covenant is as sure as any He has ever made.

This is a covenant of peace.

> *For the mountains shall depart, and the hills be removed; but my kindness shall not depart from thee, neither shall the covenant of my peace be removed, saith the* LORD *that hath mercy on thee.* (Isaiah 54:10)

The exchange made it possible for God to be at peace with man. Sin has been judged in Jesus. We have been made righteous in Him; now we have peaceful fellowship with God. He swore that His kindness and peace would not depart from us.

If someone came on the scene and proclaimed that God was going to judge the world by water, we all would quickly realize the error. God says, "As surely as I will never destroy the world with water, I will not be angry with you; I will not rebuke you; My kindness will not depart from you; the covenant of peace will not be removed from you, because *I am a merciful God.*"

The covenant with Noah was sealed with a rainbow. The covenant of peace was sealed in the blood of Jesus. If God violates this covenant, then He has denounced the blood of Jesus. A violation of this covenant would be total rejection of the blood, the death, and the resurrection of His Son. But this covenant is sure.

God will never destroy the world by water. So what would you do if your favorite preacher, the person you trust most, stands up and says, "I've heard from God. He's going to destroy the world by water." Regardless of how much you love and trust that person, you would not receive that message. You would confidently look back to the covenant God made with Noah. You would stand on God's Word. What if that same person stood up and said, "God's not going to judge the world with water, but He is going to destroy one nation by water"? Again, the error would be obvious. What if that person said, "Well, God's not going to destroy the world by water, but He's so mad He's going to drown one person"? Again, the error would be obvious.

The reason the error would be obvious is that we all know about the covenant with Noah. Unfortunately, we are more aware of the covenant with Noah than we are of the covenant with Jesus. Ignorance causes people to go into captivity and bondage. Our top priority as Christians should be to know the new covenant. We are to live, worship, and minister by this covenant.

God swore that He would be at peace with mankind. This means both believers and nonbelievers. Jesus did not appease the wrath of God for the sins of the church. He appeased the wrath of God for the world. So at the present time, God is judging no man for his sin.

There surely will be a time of judgment for those who are not found in Christ, but today, God is judging no man. This covenant of peace is sure.

Righteousness is what makes all of this possible. *"In righteousness shalt thou be established"* (Isaiah 54:14). Verse 17 is quick to point out, *"And their righteousness is of me, saith the LORD"*—not the righteousness of man that comes by works, but the righteousness of faith that comes by the Lord Jesus.

As God said in Isaiah 40:2, *"Speak ye comfortably to Jerusalem, and cry unto her, that her warfare is accomplished, that her iniquity is pardoned."* The war is over. God saw the problem, and He did all it would take to solve it through Jesus. Because this thing is of God, it is sure and consistent.

What about the message that says God is judging you? What about the message that makes one feel God is the source of all his pain and affliction? Isaiah 54:17 says, *"And every tongue that shall rise against thee in judgment thou shalt condemn."* *The Emphasized Bible* says it this way: *"And every tongue that riseth against thee in judgment, shalt thou prove to be lawless."* The tongue that pronounces the judgment of God on man is a lawless tongue. It does not speak in line with the new covenant. We can no more accept the message of God's wrath being poured out on man at this time than we could accept the prophecy of another worldwide flood. This is why the angels sang, *"Glory to God in the highest, and* **on earth peace, good will toward men**" (Luke 2:14, emphasis added).

The message that says God is judging someone before the time of judgment is as absurd as someone saying God is going to judge the world by water. We have a sure word and a sure covenant sealed in the blood of Jesus.

There is a rationale, however, that says, "If I violate my covenant, then God is freed from His side of the covenant." We must understand that God did not establish His covenant with us; He established it with Jesus. In order for this covenant to be broken, Jesus must fail. He did not fail. He finished every aspect of the work. Thus this covenant is established, it is settled, it is sure, and it is unchangeable.

Galatians 3:16 explains, *"Now to Abraham and his seed were the promises made. He saith not, And to seeds, as of many; but as of one, And to thy seed, which is Christ."* The promises were made to Jesus. The covenant was with Jesus. Because I am in Him, I qualify to participate in the covenant.

We accept that God made a covenant with Noah that benefits all of us. We would never think that our actions could alter the covenant made with Noah. Likewise, our actions cannot alter the covenant made with Jesus.

We have a covenant of peace, and it is sure. It is sealed with the blood of Jesus.

# Thirteen

&

# The Love of God

## Thirteen

### ❧

# The Love of God

*And we have known and believed the love that God hath to*
*us. God is love; and he that dwelleth in love dwelleth in God,*
*and God in him.*
—1 John 4:16

*T*he apostle John not only believed in God's love, but he
also had experienced it. He had tapped into the greatest power in existence—the love of God.

When I was first saved, I wanted desperately to know
God's power. I wanted to see God's mighty acts. Like Elijah,
I expected to know God in the earthquake, in the fire, and in
the wind. I soon discovered that you could see all these things
and still not know God. Knowing God's power soon became
secondary to knowing God.

You will grasp the fullness of God's power only to the
degree that you grasp the fullness of His love. Paul understood this when he prayed for the Ephesians to be

> *rooted and grounded in love,* [that they] *may be able*
> *to comprehend with all saints what is the breadth, and*
> *length, and depth, and height; and to know the love of*

*Christ, which passeth knowledge, that ye might be filled with all the fulness of God.* (Ephesians 3:17–19)

Paul knew that the key to being filled with God's power was knowing and believing His love.

Love is the motivating factor behind all that God does. More than anything else, God is love. Therefore, you know and understand God only by understanding the God-kind of love. This is the major key to miracles, healing, faith, and peace.

When I pray for the sick, cast out devils, or intercede, it is not a matter of my trying to work up a super faith. It is not a matter of trying to change God's mind. It is not a matter of the individual having a good enough life to receive. All I know is the great love of God that has already given the very best He has to offer—Jesus. I do not trust in my super faith; I trust in God's super love. My faith is simply a response to the love and integrity of God.

In Romans 8:32–34 Paul presented a series of questions that should cause us to realize that God is not the one causing our problems. *"He that spared not his own Son, but delivered him up for us all, how shall he not with him also freely give us all things?"* (v. 32). In Paul's first question he reminded us that God has already given the best. Why would God withhold anything from us after He has already given us the best He has?

He also pointed out that God freely gives all these things. We received Jesus freely. We were not worthy. Our lives were not good enough. So why would God require us to earn any-thing else? If anything should have been earned, surely it would have been the right to become sons of God. But that was given freely. When Jesus sent out His disciples, He said, *"Heal the sick, cleanse the lepers, raise the dead, cast out devils:* ***freely ye have received, freely give****"* (Matthew 10:8, emphasis added). Jesus placed no price on His goodness, then or now.

It seems we are afraid that if we preach a free Gospel, the undeserving will receive. That is exactly the point; the undeserving need to experience the love of God. When the undeserving experience the love of God, that kindness will bring them to a change of mind (repentance) about God. When they taste and see that the Lord is good, they may not want to go back to the pigpen to eat.

Paul continued to ask, *"Who shall lay any thing to the charge of God's elect? It is God that justifieth"* (Romans 8:33). The original language says, "Who shall bring an accusation against the chosen ones of God? Will God who acquits them?" God is not looking for fault in us, so the obvious answer is no. If God is the One who acquitted us, if God is the One who justifies, if God is the One who makes us righteous, why would He turn around and bring a charge or accusation against us? God is not the faultfinder.

Think of it! God gave me the righteousness that I have. I do not come before Him with my righteousness; I come before Him with the righteousness He gave Jesus. Therefore, if God finds fault with me, He has found fault with His own work. I am His workmanship, created in Christ Jesus. (See Ephesians 2:10.)

Why would God find fault with His own work? Obviously, He doesn't. That means the feelings of not measuring up and the sense of fear and uncertainty I feel about approaching God are the products of my own heart. God is not finding fault with me.

It is obvious that if I sin, my heart will condemn me. I need to listen to my heart. I need to change the behavior that is robbing me of my confidence before God. But God is greater than my heart. My heart tells me that I need to change my behavior to live in proper relationship with other people. The finished work of Jesus, though, tells me that God still loves and accepts me. It tells me I can come before Him with boldness and get help, even though I may have problems.

Paul continued, *"Who is he that condemneth? It is Christ that died, yea rather, that is risen again, who is even at the right hand of God, who also maketh intercession for us"* (Romans 8:34). Again, Paul pointed out the absurdity that condemnation, faultfinding, and judgment would come from the Lord Jesus. Why would He find fault if He is the one who died for us? Obviously, He would not.

If Jesus is for me, He cannot be against me. He would not be for me in the presence of God and against me in my presence. The feelings of condemnation, the expectations of judgment, are not from Him. Jesus is for me, not against me.

Although most Christians agree with that, they draw the line when a person sins. It is easy to believe God loves us when we do right, but few people believe that God loves us when we do wrong. First John 2:1 says, *"My little children, these things write I unto you, that ye sin not."* It is obvious that God does not want us to sin, but the verse does not stop there. *"And if any man sin, we have an advocate with the Father, Jesus Christ the righteous."* It does not say that God judges us when we sin. It does not say Jesus will accuse us. It says that when we sin, Jesus is still our Advocate. An advocate is one who is for you, not against you. Even when you sin, Jesus is still for you. He's not the one who condemns you. He's the One who helps you come out of sin.

The Bible says satan, not Jesus, is the accuser of the brethren. Condemnation does not help anyone come out of sin. Rather, it destroys confidence and self-worth. It paralyzes the confidence that God wants to help us. Condemnation is the strongest tool the devil has against the believer. If he can make you believe that God is against you, he can separate you from the only One who can help you.

We have been so conditioned to think God that is the source of our difficulties. When trouble comes, our first thought is very often, "Oh, no, what have I done now? Why is God doing this to me?" Isaiah 54:15 says, *"They shall surely gather together, but not by me."* Or as Jeremiah prophesied, *"And they shall fight against thee; but they shall not prevail against thee; for I am with thee, saith the LORD, to deliver thee"* (Jeremiah 1:19).

Now, if God is the Deliverer, He cannot be the destroyer. If God is for you, He cannot be against you. The New Testament says it this way: *"Let no man say when he is tempted, I am tempted of God: for God cannot be tempted with evil, neither tempteth he any man"* (James 1:13). The word *"tempted"* means "solicitated to evil, trial, or tribulation," or "scrutinized." Do not say that your trials are from God. When you feel you are being scrutinized, do not say it is God. God is not looking you over for fault. He has made you righteous in Jesus.

We have made God out to be the bad guy. The world does not want to come to the God we have presented to them. Most people (Christians) feel that it is easier to be a sinner than to be a Christian. But be assured, the God we have shown the world is not the God Jesus showed to the world. Either He was wrong about God, or we are.

I remember sharing about the love of God with an alcoholic. I assured him of God's love and mercy. As he sat weeping, he suddenly said, "Let me see your Bible." I handed it to him and asked, "What are you looking for?" He said, "I wanted to see if this was the same Bible the other preachers use." He continued, "I've never heard of the God you're talking about." Here was a man who lived in the Bible Belt of America. He grew up in church, yet he had never heard of God's love.

God does not have a double standard. He does not require us to love and yet exempt Himself from loving. He is the Author of love. All real love comes from God. His love was demonstrated in the fact that He sent Jesus to die for us. We did not deserve it and did not even want it, yet in His love, He sent His only Son.

When Jesus comes in us, He brings the *zoe* life of God. All the healing, power, prosperity, and fullness of God are in you in Christ. As you become persuaded in the love of God, you will allow His life (*zoe*) to flow into you with confidence, joy, and thanksgiving.

# Fourteen

❧

# Good News Faith

*Fourteen*

℘

# Good News Faith

The Gospel of peace is the only source for building real faith. For years we have taken Romans 10:17 to mean, "If you keep hearing the Word, faith will come." There was a time when I believed and taught it that way. That, however, is not what the Scripture says, and history certainly does not bear it out.

If just hearing the Word would build faith, why aren't all people working miracles, healing the sick, and raising the dead? Why don't all people who hear the Word trust God? If faith (trust) comes from just hearing the Word, it would be a simple thing to bring all people to a life-changing faith in God. But many people who read the Bible become fearful. They often pull away from God. The majority of people sitting in churches don't really trust God with every aspect of their lives. Yet they are hearing the Word.

Romans 10:17 says, *"So then faith cometh by hearing, and hearing by the word of God."* To understand this, or any Scripture, we must understand it in light of the context. The context for understanding this passage is the previous ten chapters of Romans, which are all about faith-righteousness.

In Romans 10:13, the Scripture begins to get specific: *"For whosoever shall call upon the name of the Lord shall be saved."* It then explains the progression whereby a person is compelled to call upon the name of the Lord. Verse 14 explains that he will not call on the name of the Lord if he does not believe.

The Bible goes on to say that people will not believe if they have not heard. What you hear about God will determine if you call on Him. If what you hear makes you believe that God loves and accepts you, you will confidently call upon Him. If what you hear makes you unsure of God's love for you, you will not call on Him with confident trust (faith).

Then the Scripture asks, *"How shall they hear without a preacher?"* (v. 14). Regardless of what the Bible says, the preacher you hear will affect the way you hear (understand) the Word. A man once came to Jesus and asked Him a question. Jesus' reply was not what one would expect. He asked the man, *"What is written in the law? how readest thou?"* (Luke 10:26). Jesus asked him two questions: first, What does the Word say? and second, How do you interpret that?

What the Word says and how we read or interpret it can be worlds apart. We have been tempered and molded to see God the way the preacher sees Him. This is why it is so essential to read the Bible for yourself and to develop your own concepts of God through the Word and personal involvement.

In Luke 8:18, Jesus warns, *"Take heed therefore **how** ye hear"* (emphasis added). How you hear is as important as what you hear. If you hear a promise of God, it is absolutely true. But if you place a wrong stipulation on receiving that promise, you have taken what could bring life and turned it to bring death.

I must allow the Word to speak for itself. I must not place what seems to be reasonable interpretation on the Word of God apart from it having a foundation in the new covenant. I can't look to the old covenant to understand how God will operate under the new covenant, although it may seem reasonable and logical. To do so is to reject the validity of the new covenant.

I must realize that the person who preaches the Word to me affects my hearing. I am partaking of his perceptions and preferences. Thus the Bible says, *"How shall they preach, except they be sent?"* (Romans 10:15). There are too many who are not sent forth with the message of the new covenant. They have run forth out of their own zeal. They are anxious to perpetuate their own perceptions, but they are not sent with the Gospel of peace.

The whole of Romans 10:15 says,

> *And how shall they preach, except they be sent? as it is written, How beautiful are the feet of them that preach the gospel of peace, and bring glad tidings of good things!*

Not every preacher has beautiful feet. Not every preacher walks in the pathway of peace. Scripture says those who *"preach the gospel of peace,"* those who *"bring glad tidings of good things,"* are the ones who are sent.

Unfortunately, not all the preachers who have gone forth believe the report. They do not believe there is a covenant of peace. Therefore, they preach a message of fear and condemnation. Thus we have the fulfillment of Romans 10:16: *"But they have not all obeyed the gospel. For Esaias saith, Lord, who hath believed our report?"*

Faith does not come from hearing the Word in general. Faith comes when we hear the Good News, the glad tidings of the Gospel of peace. Hearing the Gospel of peace will build faith (trust). Hearing bad news about works, law, and performance will destroy confident trust (faith). The message of peace makes one run to God; the message of judgment makes one run away from God.

Hebrews 11:1 says, *"Now faith is the substance of things hoped for, the evidence of things not seen."* Real faith is always the product of hope. The word *hope* in the original language means "a confident expectation of good things." A confident expectation of bad things produces fear. A confident expectation of good things always produces faith.

Expectation of good things should be the general view of all Christians. In every situation we should be expecting good things from God. We will never do that if we are hearing teaching that labels God as the source of all our hurts, trials, problems, and tribulations. That kind of teaching promotes the expectation of bad things from God. The Bible calls that *fear.* According to Hebrews 11:1, faith cannot exist where there is no hope (confident expectation of good).

Even faith itself is turned to law if you have a wrong concept of God. I have seen many Christians trying to change God's mind and earn His acceptance with their faith. That is nothing more than works. It is not faith at all. Faith functions on the basis of promises, not works. Faith trusts God because He is good. It does not try to get Him to do good. Faith knows God is good.

We have wrongly been taught that faith is what we do to get God to respond. If we must do anything to get God to respond, then we are in works. Faith is not what we do to get God to respond; faith is our response to what God has already done in Jesus. If we must provoke God to do something, then we do not believe it is already done in Jesus. If we know that

God has given all provision in Jesus, then we have a confident expectation in this life.

Either hope or fear will rule our lives in every situation. If we are not confidently expecting good, then we are in fear or worry. This basic concept we have of God affects our faith more than anything else. We can learn all the techniques or methods of working faith, but without the confident expectation of good, faith will not come.

The wrong concept of God generally comes from the inability to separate the old and new covenants. Most Christians have mixed the two together and are trying to relate to God on the basis of a perverted covenant. In Psalm 78:37 God explains that Israel's problem was a heart problem: *"For their heart was not right with him, neither were they stedfast in his covenant."* Likewise, we are not steadfast in this new covenant.

Because we are not steadfast in the new covenant, we are quick to pervert it by mixing it with the old. We are continually looking to the Old Testament to understand how God will relate to man. Since our beliefs are not based in the new covenant, we come to God with certain predetermined perspectives. These perspectives determine how we hear, read, interpret, and understand the Word of God.

I once heard a story about a young boy who sat on the seashore and watched the boats going by. As he watched, he realized that the wind blew only in one direction, but the boats went in every direction. He asked a wise elderly man, "How is it the wind blows only one direction, but the boats sail in every direction?" The wise old man answered, "It is not the direction of the wind that determines the direction of the boat; it is the setting of the sail."

Likewise, in our lives, it is not the direction of the Word we read as much as it is the direction of the beliefs of our hearts.

We have set our sails through our traditions. Those traditions can make the Word of God to be of no effect in our lives, just as it did for the Pharisees in the time of Jesus (Mark 7:13).

Apart from the Gospel of peace, we won't have the hope that brings faith. Jesus read the same Scripture as the Pharisees, yet He found God to be a healer and miracle worker. He found God to be a merciful Father, ready to forgive and restore men. The Pharisees read the Scripture and found an angry God who would weigh men down with heavy religious burdens. What was the difference? The setting of the sail.

You see, you find what you look for. If you believe God to be mean and judgmental, or just hard to please, you will find Scriptures to reinforce that. But if, like Jesus, you see God as a loving Father, you will find the promises that give hope.

Proverbs 10:29 says, *"The way of the* LORD *is strength to the upright: but destruction...to the workers of iniquity."* According to the condition of your heart, the word that sets one man free can make you bound. The word that shows one man the love of God can show you something different. Therefore, we should be careful who or what is forming our view of God.

Our view of God is continually being developed. We should guard our hearts against anything that would cause us to lose confidence and trust in God. The Bible says in Romans 1:17, *"For therein* [in the Gospel] *is the righteousness of God revealed from faith to faith: as it is written, The just shall live by faith."* Everything I hear and believe should support the view of faith-righteousness and thereby cause me to trust God.

# Fifteen

&

# Sowing and Reaping

# Fifteen
## ❧

# Sowing and Reaping

*M*any people fear that the Gospel of peace will promote a liberal lifestyle. It seems that the negative mind sees retribution as the only way to curtail sin. Through this fear of people taking advantage of God, we have, with good intentions, withheld the truth. Paul, however, said that he was not ashamed of the Gospel (Good News). He realized it to be the power of God unto salvation (Romans 1:16). He knew that only the good news of faith-righteousness could bring about the kind of salvation God has provided and expects.

Paul faced persecution for his message. In the book of Romans, he pointed out that he had been accused of encouraging sin. In the book of First Corinthians, he had to defend his message and his apostleship. In the book of Galatians, he talked about how the Judaizers had criticized his message. They tried to bring the people out of peace and grace and into a mixture of the old and new covenants. But Paul still confidently proclaimed, "I am not ashamed of the good news of faith-righteousness."

You must realize that there will be those who feel they can take advantage of the goodness of God. Such people will be the way they are regardless of what you preach. A perverted heart will always pervert anything to self-gratification. But we cannot let the perversion of some people license us to lie. Instead of changing his message, Paul warned in Galatians 5:13, *"Only use not liberty for an occasion to the flesh."* He gave similar warnings in Corinthians. Peter warned against the same thing. We must warn, but we cannot change the truth.

Galatians 6:7 says, *"Be not deceived; God is not mocked: for whatsoever a man soweth, that shall he also reap."* The Phillips translation says it this way: *"Don't be under any illusion: you cannot make a fool of God! A man's harvest in life will depend entirely on what he sows."* AIDS is not the judgment of an angry God; neither is sickness, poverty, or all the other plagues of humanity. Some of our pains are obviously the work of the devil, but the majority of that which hurts us is the product of sinful sowing and consequent reaping.

We should warn people of the destruction of sin. We should make them realize how much pain sin can bring into a person's life. But we should never try to make them think that the pain is God's judgment against them for their sin. This life is a series of decisions. We must live with the consequences of the decisions we make. When we act independently of truth, we will reap a crop of destruction. When we make decisions based on truth, we will reap a good harvest.

The law of sowing and reaping is not a matter of God's blessings or punishment. It is just a natural law that God set in place. When you plant a crop, you can't plant just any kind of seed and get the desired results. You must plant the seed that will produce what you want.

When people realize that sin is the source of their pain, they will hate sin. Since people think God is the source of their pain, they hate God. God has not hurt anyone under the new covenant. He has set us free from the curse of the law, and He has given us the wisdom of His Word to know how to avoid painful decisions.

God has shown us how to live in victory. He has made the way possible through the Lord Jesus. If we choose to live in destruction, it is not God judging us; it is the product of our actions. Do not be deceived; the law of sowing and reaping is sure. But praise God, there is a higher law. It is the law of the Spirit of life (*zoe*) in Christ Jesus (Romans 8:2).

When we are tired of the destruction of our own way, we can turn to a loving, merciful God, receive forgiveness, and be delivered from the law of sowing and reaping. You might ask, Does this mean a person could sin, ask for forgiveness, and never suffer any penalty of his sin? Yes, if there is true repentance, confession, and turning back to the Lord. But there is an effect of sin that is more devastating than any of the afflictions that come on our flesh.

The Bible warns that we should guard our hearts with all diligence, because all the issues of life come from the heart (Proverbs 4:23). Everything your life is or will be is a product of your heart. You cannot rise above the condition of your heart. You will ultimately live out the abundance of your heart. Therefore, the most devastating effects of sin are seen in how it affects the heart.

Hebrews 3:13 says, *"But exhort one another daily, while it is called To day; lest any of you be hardened through the deceitfulness of sin."* Sin hardens the heart. It makes the heart insensitive to God. Paul warned Christians in the book of Ephesians not to live like the Gentiles do.

*This I say therefore, and testify in the Lord, that ye henceforth walk not as other Gentiles walk, in the vanity of their mind, having the understanding darkened, being alienated from the life [zoe] of God through the ignorance that is in them, because of the blindness [hardness] of their heart: who being past feeling have given themselves over.*                (Ephesians 4:17–19)

Paul warned that living in sin will darken our understanding of God, which will result in our being alienated from the life, the abundance, the *zoe* of God.

Alienation happens through ignorance of godly things, which is a product of blindness, or hardness, of heart. Even after we have received forgiveness from our sin, there is still a problem with our hearts. This problem can be solved, but it is not easily detected.

Hardness of heart refers to a callus on the heart. When one works with a hoe or shovel without gloves, he usually gets blisters on his hands. These blisters are very painful and make it difficult to go back to the same kind of activity. Similarly, when we as Christians get involved in sin, it is very painful to our hearts. Since we have a righteous nature, we can no longer sin without feeling pain. But if the person doing that yard work goes back to the same type of work, those sensitive blisters will eventually become calluses that inhibit feeling pain. Likewise, one who continues in sin will callous his heart to the point of not being able to feel or detect the work, conviction, and direction of the Holy Spirit.

As Paul said in verse 19, he will be past feeling. Lenski says this is "to cease to feel the pain of conviction." Now the man continues in the sin, not realizing the destruction that is being created. Often, one even reaches a point of feeling that his sin is acceptable to God. After all, he does not feel any discomfort.

That lack of pain in the heart is not God's approval, however. It is the devastating, deceitful effect of sin.

Hebrews 3:12 warns, *"Take heed, brethren, lest there be in any of you an evil heart of unbelief, in departing from the living God."* The deceitfulness of sin is not obvious. The deceitfulness of sin is the inward effect on the heart. Be assured, though, a hardened heart will eventually choose to turn away from God—*and feel no pain.*

The book of Hebrews contains six strong warnings about sin. These warnings are stronger than most preachers and Christians like to admit. Basically, we are warned against apostasy. You will not find this word in the King James Version, but it is found in the original language. An apostate is one who turns away, never to return. An apostate is not one who loses his salvation; he is one who throws it away.

We have security in Christ, but we also have a freedom of choice. No one gets up in the morning and says, "Hey, I think I'll throw away my relationship with God today. I believe I'll turn from God so I can spend eternity in hell." No, it does not happen that way. Rather, through a long, deceitful process, sin can bring us to that point. And the reason it is so hard to turn around is that *we feel no pain!*

If you are backslidden, do not assume you have reached this point. As long as you are alive, you can turn around. But hear the strength of this warning: If you stay in sin, you may ultimately throw God away.

God never quits loving you when you are in sin. Jesus never turns against you. He will forever be for you (1 John 2:1). But you will turn against Him. So, along with the message of peace, we have to present the warnings. You cannot take advantage of God. He won't get you, but your sin will.

We also must understand the effects of sin in this life. Although God is merciful, people are not. Long after we have experienced God's forgiveness, we must still live with the way our sins have affected other people. There may be a lack of trust. There may be anger. There may be those who will never forgive what we have done to them. This is only one of the many painful aspects of sowing and reaping.

Sixteen

&

# A Relationship of Love

# Sixteen

൸

# A Relationship of Love

*W*hen I first began to attend church, I heard all the talk about making Jesus my personal Savior and having a personal relationship with the Lord. But as I began to fellowship with those who used this terminology, I found that they did not have a personal relationship with Jesus. They had a personal relationship with their ideas, doctrines, and beliefs.

They were good people, and they were no doubt saved. However, what I saw and was taught about God was anything but a relationship. Relationships require time and effort, two things most people are not willing and sometimes not able to give. I have actually had people say, "Just give me some rules, and I'll keep them." Rules require very little, but Jesus came to restore us to a relationship with the Father. This relationship is to be built on love and trust.

In the book of John, as Jesus was spending His last hours teaching His disciples, He explained that He would die, but that He would be raised from the dead. He promised that after His resurrection He would send the Holy Spirit, the Comforter, the Counselor, the Spirit of Grace and Truth. He explained that He would be to us all that Jesus had been while He was here on earth, with one exception: The Comforter would live inside us. He would draw us into a relationship with the Father from our hearts.

Jesus said, *"If you love Me, keep My commandments"* (John 14:15 NKJV). Fear will cause a person to obey someone he hates or despises. A slave has no choice but to obey his master for fear of reprisals. But Jesus said, *"If you love Me, keep My commandments."* Our obedience should be the product of love, not fear.

As a young boy in Tennessee, I had a world of problems. I was full of anger and bitterness. I would curse, steal, fight, and do all the things a mean little boy would do. I loved my mother, but my home environment was so bad I hated being there. I made bad grades in school, and I had no interest in improving myself.

The one redeeming relationship in my life was with my uncle. When he came home from the military, I was staying with my grandmother, and he took an interest in me. He was my hero. He was everything I wanted to be. He had extremely high standards, and he expected me to live up to his standards, but there was no negativism in it at all. He always conveyed trust in me. He always told me I was able to do what he expected. Because he believed in me, he could get me to do, through love, what a hundred spankings had never been able to do. I did not obey him for fear of what he would do. I obeyed him because I loved him, respected him, and valued our relationship. I could not bear the idea of disappointing him with my behavior.

Similarly, when we come to know the love of God and His great goodness, we realize the value of the relationship. I do not want to do anything to displease or disappoint the One who has done so much for me. Because I love Him, I am going to walk in His Word. When I fail, I know I am not rejected. It is a wonderful thing to have a relationship with someone who has high standards, but who does not reject us when we fail to live up to those standards. The fact that someone believes in you will enable you to get up when you fall.

God does not have one standard of love for Himself and another standard for us. The love described in 1 Corinthians 13 is God's kind of love. We are required to walk in that kind of love because we are to be like God. God's love does not reject or condemn; neither does it allow us to do so. Although He is holy and perfect, He does not reject us in our imperfection. Instead, because we have an environment of peace and acceptance, we can continually draw from His strength until we do overcome.

In John 14:21, 23, Jesus said,

> *He that hath my commandments, and keepeth them, he it is that loveth me: and he that loveth me shall be loved of my Father, and I will love him, and will manifest myself to him....If a man love me, he will keep my words: and my Father will love him, and we will come unto him, and make our abode with him.*

Jesus wants to manifest Himself to you. He wants to have a personal relationship with you, one in which He and the Father come and fellowship with you, teach you, and love you. This is a relationship of the heart. It is like a marriage. In fact, the church is described as the bride of Christ. The Spirit of God led Paul to teach about husbands and wives so that we could understand the church's relationship to Jesus. I love my wife dearly, and I am not afraid of her hurting me or trying to bring me pain. She wants me to succeed and be happy. If I mistreat the person who desires so many good things for me, I am a fool.

I am not good to her out of fear of her. When my wife and I have a disagreement, she sometimes gives me the silent treatment. Although she can inflict pain by doing something like this to me, it doesn't necessarily make me stop relating properly to her. Rather, the loss of the joy, peace, and fulfillment of our relationship motivates me to make things right again. There are many good things in our relationship, and I have too much to lose by handling it improperly.

Likewise, Jesus loves me. He comforts me. When I am sick, He heals me. I never have to fear. I never have to lack because He is always there. Why should I withdraw from a relationship that means so much to me? The gratification of sin is not equal to the gratification of the relationship.

As you come to know and experience the goodness of the Lord, you will develop a loving relationship that is more precious than anything else in your life. The fulfillment of that relationship will keep you from sin. Love accomplishes far more than law. This happens only when we know and experience the love of God through an intimate, personal relationship with Him.

# Seventeen

&

# Discerning the Heart

*Seventeen*

୧୬

# Discerning the Heart

Since the heart is the most important aspect of our being, we should know more about the heart than anything else. However, we are a people void of understanding. That is why we reduce our relationship with God to rules and regulations.

Law does not allow a person to understand his own heart. A person can do all the right things for all the wrong reasons. For instance, two people can commit the same actions. One person can be sincere and honest; another can be manipulative and deceitful. On the outside they may look the same; however, on the inside were different motivations.

Nowhere does the Bible give us the right to judge the heart, or the motivation, of another. Many times I hear people say, "Oh, he has such a good heart." I often want to ask, "How do you know? And who gave you the right to pass that judgment?" Judgment belongs to the Lord. We cannot even properly judge our own hearts, much less the heart of another. The Bible says the Word of God will discern, or judge, or sift our hearts. The Word of God is the mirror that I use to understand my own heart. If I look into the Word and put it into practice with love as my motive, my deeds are revealed as light or darkness. By walking in the love described in God's Word, I put my heart to rest in God's presence and drive out all condemnation.

In recent years, I have had the opportunity to rescue many people who are coming out of a legalistic environment. When these people leave a church or pastor that kept them in line through judgment and condemnation, they fall apart. They get to the place where they do not want to go to a church, pray, tithe, or anything. Many onlookers would say, "See, this liberal message promotes sin." It is quite the opposite. The mercy, truth, and light of God do not promote sin; they expose it. What a shock it is to these people to find that when they had no one to "browbeat" them, they stopped serving God. When the element of fear was removed, they found that they were not really in love with God. Many people spend a lifetime going through the motions and never understanding why they have no real, inner victory in living for God.

You see, these are not people who are in a loving relationship with Jesus, a relationship in which He and the Father come to them and manifest themselves. They are living under law and know very little of the goodness of God. Many of these people have never experienced the real repentance that brings a change of mind and heart. There has been only the repentance that abstains for fear of the results. These people, though doing good works, are backslidden in their hearts. They serve God, but not from the heart. It is lip service. I am not challenging their salvation, but I do question the joy of their salvation.

Proverbs 14:14 says, *"The backslider in heart shall be filled with his own ways."* The condition of your heart is filling your life with good or bad things. All may look good on the outside, but what's on the inside? Every person I have known who grasps this message goes through a major upheaval in the inner man.

I sat one day talking with a man who had come from a very performance-oriented background. For a number of years he had been a "high achiever." He was one of the up-and-coming young men in a rather large congregation.

As he sat talking to me, he said, "This just isn't working. Since I've been hearing this message I haven't been as dedicated. I don't pray as much. I don't read my Bible as much. I don't witness as much." My simple response was, "It sounds like it's working to me." "How could that be?" he asked.

I said, "How many of those things that you did, for all those years, were done because you loved God and you loved people? Or how many of those things were done because you were trying to get on staff? Or were you possibly trying to gain the favor of the leaders?"

We sat staring at one another for a few long moments of silence. He dropped his head into his hands and began to cry. "Most of it was to get on staff," he responded. "I wanted the oversight to approve of me."

I believe in living a productive life; I just prefer that people do it out of love. I see people like this young man go through these difficult changes. I see them struggle to get back in touch with God. It is so hard to find reality and relationship after so many years of performance and hypocrisy. But then I see these people begin to bear fruit. I see them enter into a joy and peace that is beyond anything they have ever known.

Love demands proper attitudes and motives. Love does not work by law and obligation. The Gospel of peace requires a right heart. Be assured, this message will produce havoc in a person whose heart is not right before the Lord. If this message produces the attitude of loose or ungodly living, you have a heart problem. If you feel that you can take advantage of God's mercy and forgiveness, you have a heart problem. The problem is not the message. Remember, *"The way of the LORD is strength to the upright: but destruction...to the workers of iniquity"* (Proverbs 10:29).

The heart is the seat of our emotions and our will. Emotions can come from different sources. They can be stimulated from the spirit or from the flesh. Emotions can be very deceitful. Many people live for God, yet they are robbed of confidence because of condemnation. Others live for self and deceive themselves into believing they are right before God. So emotions are not a stable indicator of the condition of our heart. First John 3:18–21 tells us how to assure or persuade our hearts before God. Verses 18–19 say that the only way to know we are in truth is by loving in both word and deed. Walking in love can settle the issue when our hearts condemn us. Works do not earn me a position or favor with God. But the fruit that comes forth because of my relationship with God helps to assure my heart. It becomes a mirror to my inner man.

When my heart does not condemn me, I have confidence, and I receive whatsoever I ask. Confidence is an important part of faith. I must first have a confident expectation of God. I must have confidence of my own standing before God.

First John 3:22 says, *"And whatsoever we ask, we receive of him, because we keep his commandments, and do those things that are pleasing in his sight."* One would quickly say, "See, you must keep the commandments to get your prayers answered." Remember, the context is walking in love. Keeping the commandments does not earn answered prayer. Instead, keeping His commandments assures our hearts.

Verse 23 goes on to say, *"And this is his commandment, That we should believe on the name of his Son Jesus Christ, and love one another, as he gave us commandment."* Believing on Jesus and walking in love fulfills the commandments of the Lord. Therefore, the way I live, in regard to my belief on the Lord Jesus and walking in love, reveals the condition of my heart. I don't have to relate to the Lord and His people in the "right" way in order to avoid judgment. They are things I do because of the love of God in my heart.

When the threat of judgment is removed, we have the opportunity to see what is really in a person's heart. If you hear this message of love and peace and feel it gives you a license to sin, your heart has been revealed. Now you know why you have struggled in the past. Now you know what you have really been dealing with. Truth will reveal the condition of the heart. It will sort out the real motives and intentions. *"For the word of God…is a discerner of the thoughts and intents of the heart"* (Hebrews 4:12).

Eighteen

&

# Bringing Forth the Heart

*Eighteen*

ೞ

# Bringing Forth the Heart

*I*n our negative thinking, we have assumed that the Lord could change man only through harsh, painful dealings. But, praise God, that is not the case. Only a fool has to learn the hard way. God does not relate to us as fools, but as sons. Under the old covenant, He had to deal with man from the outside. He used negative circumstances to urge people in the right direction. He brought about pain and affliction to make one realize the error of his way. However, that is not needed for the pure of heart.

Even under the old covenant, God tried every way possible to help man avoid ultimate destruction. Because man was not regenerated, God could not speak to his heart. He always dealt with man from the outside. There were parents, elders, teachers, prophets, and others who would instruct a person in the way. There was the teaching of the Word of God. There were many avenues for man to hear instruction, learn, and change. A wise man would hear a rebuke and learn. A wise man could be taught. A wise man did not have to experience pain to heed his ways. This is why Proverbs 10:8 says, *"The wise in heart will receive commandments: but a prating fool shall fall."*

A foolish man is very different. Proverbs 19:29 tells us, *"Judgments are prepared for scorners, and stripes for the back of fools."* A fool is one who will not learn by instruction. He will learn only from the consequences. Pain is the only hope for the man who will not read the Word and believe. Consequences are the only deterrents to a person who will not be led by the Holy Spirit.

What God did on the outside under the law, He now does on the inside in the heart. I know by experience that there is nothing more painful than a healthy conscience that is pricked by sin. I know the severity of going in a direction that is not pleasing to the Lord. The pain I feel is not judgment, though; the pain is what a renewed nature feels when it violates that nature.

When Jesus came into our lives, He made us new creations. We no longer have a sin nature. We are no longer able to live in sin comfortably. We are now righteous. The Holy Spirit is continually convicting us that we are righteous. Consequently, we are not compatible with sin.

Besides the pain of our conscience, sin also brings pain into our lives from several sources. On of the main areas sin causes pain and difficulty is in our relationships. Its effects destroy meaningful relationships and separate us from those we love.

We must never falsely assume that all the pain we experience from our foolish or sinful ways is the wrath of God. God said sin would kill us. If we do not believe that and do not avoid sin, we will learn about the pain of sin as an unteachable fool does. God does not add pain to our sin, either. Rather, He draws us out of sin and gives us the strength to change.

How does the Lord change and chasten us? The word *chasten* means "to train a child." Until the time of Augustine, *chasten* was a positive word. It described a father developing and compelling his child in the right direction. Augustine redefined the word under the assumption that in Christianity it had to have a harsher meaning. Therefore, we still have a negative view of God's dealings with His children.

The book of Hebrews says,

> *My son, despise not thou the chastening of the Lord, nor faint when thou art rebuked of him: for whom the Lord loveth he chasteneth, and scourgeth every son whom he receiveth.*                                   (Hebrews 12:5–6)

This passage is quoted from the book of Proverbs, which goes on to say, *"For whom the LORD loveth he correcteth; even as a father the son in whom he delighteth"* (Proverbs 3:12).

It does not say the Lord chastens as the father who hates his child. He chastens as a father who delights in his child. God delights in you because you are in Jesus, not because of your works. Because we are in Jesus, we have the high calling of being conformed to the likeness of Jesus (Romans 8:29). This is God's will for us; this is our high calling. God wants to make us just like Jesus. To accomplish this, God deals with our hearts. The change is a work of His grace in our hearts.

Proverbs 17:3 says, *"The fining pot is for silver, and the furnace for gold: but the LORD trieth the hearts."* In order to make gold and silver pure, it must be put in the furnace. The heat causes the precious metals to separate from the impurities and come forth as treasure. As the Scripture points out, the furnace does this, *"but...."* It does not say the furnace does this *and* the Lord tries the heart. If the conjunction were an *and,* the sentence would mean that the Lord does the same thing as the furnace. Instead, it says *"but."* Although it takes the furnace to make the metals pure, it takes the Lord to make the heart pure. The word *"trieth"* means "to bring forth." What

God does in you does not come by the furnace; it comes from the heart. The way God purifies us is to *bring forth* our hearts. If God can get our hearts pure, then our lives will be pure.

In Psalm 51:6, David acknowledged, *"Behold, thou desirest truth in the inward parts: and in the hidden part thou shalt make me to know wisdom."* After his experience with Bathsheba, David realized that God desired more than good works. He desired truth in the heart.

Change that comes from the heart abides. It governs our every action. It is second nature. It is effortless to walk in the beliefs of the heart. Change on the outside is nothing more than behavioral modification. That change will last only as long as we put forth effort. Its motive cannot be trusted. God wants a heart change in us.

Be assured, when we sin and suffer the consequences of sowing and reaping, we learn as fools do. I must say, although it is hard, it is better to learn as a fool than not to learn at all. Many times I have seen my children headed for difficulty. I usually warn them and suggest the steps to divert the problem. If they are wise, they heed my counsel. If they are foolish, they go ahead anyway. The Bible says, *"The simple pass on, and are punished* [destroyed]*"* (Proverbs 22:3). I am not going to let my children be destroyed, so I do not follow this same rule in extremely severe situations. But when at all possible, when they will not listen to counsel, I will let them make the wrong decision. When they begin to suffer the hardship of their decisions, they become very teachable. I could *make* them do the right thing, but then they would never grow up. I could get the desired results on the outside, but I want to see them change on the inside.

Similarly, when we stray, it can become a learning experience. God can work in us in any situation, and He will; but be assured, He did not bring the hardship. His desire is for us to be teachable and changeable through fellowship and communion with Him.

John 15:2 says, *"And every branch that beareth fruit, he purgeth it, that it may bring forth more fruit."* I have heard some "horror" sermons about God taking out His big clippers and cutting away at our lives. What is worse, I have preached some of those sermons. In verse 3 of that same chapter, Jesus continues, *"Now ye are clean through the word which I have spoken unto you."* The word *"purgeth"* in the Greek has the same root word as *clean*. Jesus did not purge His disciples by creating hardship and disaster; He did it through the Word that He spoke to them. Likewise, He cleanses, purges, chastises, and brings forth our hearts *by His Word.*

The parable of the sower in Mark 4 clearly states that the purpose of affliction and persecution is to steal the Word. Persecutions do not make us grow. Operating the Word, walking with God, and resisting temptation will make us grow up in the midst of affliction and persecution.

When my children spurn my advice, I do not reject them. I am sorry for them because I know the results of their actions will bring them only pain. If I reject them, they will have no place to go when they fail. If I love them, accept them, and try to help them, they will have the confidence and freedom to come back to me when they realize the error of their decision.

The Bible says we should come to the throne of grace in our time of need. My time of need is usually when I have failed or when I am in sin. If I believe I am rejected by God, I will not have the confidence to come to Him in my time of need. Even if I do come to Him, I will not feel free to receive His forgiveness and restoration.

Grace is a divine influence that works in one's heart to make him able to do the will of God. I do not come to the throne of grace and get a whipping. I come to the throne of grace and get mercy and find grace *to help.*

In that environment of peace, love, and acceptance, God works in my heart. In my heart, He changes me and makes me able to overcome the things that have placed me in need. Hebrews 4:16 says God wants to help in my time of need. Maybe it is time we reexamine our view and opinion of God. It is time we find the God whom Jesus showed and demonstrated. Maybe it is time we let His love, mercy, and grace help us out of our problems. We should put forth every effort to allow the Lord to work in our hearts to produce real change from within.

# Nineteen

❧

# The Heart of
the Father

# Nineteen

## &

# The Heart of the Father

O ne of the first parables I ever heard after salvation was the parable of the Prodigal Son. Although I was taught much valuable truth about the wayward son, I have since found the emphasis of this parable to be the forgiveness of the father.

In Luke 15, Jesus was surrounded by publicans and sinners. These people were unreachable by the Pharisees. Their message of judgment and legalism had no appeal to these people who were captives of their sinful lifestyles. Instead of rejoicing because someone was finally reaching these people, the religious leaders found this to be a reproach. *"This man receiveth sinners, and eateth with them"* (v. 2), they complained.

Jesus responded to their murmurings with a series of parables. The first parable—the one of the lost sheep—showed the Father's desire to reach those who had gone astray. He showed the Father's concern and ultimate joy over the repentance of one sinner. *"I say unto you, that likewise joy shall be in heaven over one sinner that repenteth, more than over ninety and nine just persons, which need no repentance"* (Luke 15:7).

In the third parable (Luke 15:11–32)—that of the Prodigal Son—Jesus clearly shows the heart of the forgiving Father, the fear of the one who fails, and the criticism of the self-righteous. The parable begins with the younger son taking his inheritance and going to the world. It is noteworthy that this is a son; this is not a foreigner. This is a child of God who has an inheritance. He totally abuses the good things of God.

While he is in the world, a famine strikes and leaves the backslider in want. Now, this famine is not the product of the Father. God does not create this situation. John 10:10 is clear that the thief comes to steal, kill, and destroy. After he lures us out into the world and destroys our confidence through sin, he then attacks. As the accuser of the brethren, he convinces us that God cannot love us or forgive us. He convinces us that it would be wrong to run back to the Father just because we are in trouble. In fact, if he can convince us that God is the one who is punishing us, he can get us to turn totally against God.

Like most of us who fall, this young man did not turn immediately to his father. He joined himself to a citizen of that country. He went to the world for help. He did not have the confidence to return to his father. What he thought he would receive and what he actually encountered when he eventually did return home were two different things.

Despite his credentials, he found himself feeding the swine of this citizen of the world. There was nothing more contemptible to a Jew than swine. That is the ultimate goal of the devil for you: shame, humiliation, and loss of identity. However, the prodigal was still the son of a wealthy man. He still had a home and identity. The only thing that stood in his way was his improper thinking about his father.

Luke 15:17 reads, *"When he came to himself."* This man had to begin to deal with the truth. Until this time, he was the product of wrong thinking about his father. He thought surely there could be no return for him. He thought his father would reject him. He thought many negative things that were not based on fact.

Most of our decisions are not based on fact. They are based on our perception of the facts. This is why the devil works so hard to establish religious perversion. If he can promote error, he can keep you from freedom. (See John 8:32.) The greatest error that permeates the church today is a carryover from the Dark Ages, when the Catholic Church used fear and judgment to control the masses. They held the people in darkness and deception by perverting the truth about God.

The judgment message is a product of that era. Until the church is free from that message, it cannot return to the Father. Since most people assume God to be the source of their problems, they never "come to themselves" as this young man did. Fortunately, although persecution and affliction are works of the devil designed to steal the Word from us, many of us do come to our senses (Mark 4:14–17).

One thing this young man had on his side was that he knew how good it was to be in his father's household. Unfortunately, many Christians have never fully realized or experienced the goodness of God. I have heard many Christians make this statement: "I had it better before I got saved. At least then I didn't have all these trials and testings." If you do not know the goodness of God, you cannot "come to yourself" as this man did. You have to know the truth before you can remember it. If your thoughts of God are negative, you will keep running away every time you fail.

Although this young man did not understand the complete truth, he did remember how good it was to live in his father's home. "Even the hired servants have it better than this," he reasoned. In Luke 15:17–19, he prepares his statement. What a contrast between what he says and what the father says! What a difference between what he expected and what he experienced!

When he returned to the father, he did not hear a list of his failures. The father had compassion, not judgment. The father did not hesitate for one moment. While the son returned with head hanging down, the father ran to meet him. Before a word of explanation was given, the father gave him a kiss of love and acceptance.

The son said, *"I have sinned...and am no more worthy"* (v. 21). The father said, *"Bring forth the best"* (v. 22). Although repentance is absolutely necessary, we must know beyond all doubt that the Father will meet us with a kiss and restore us to His best.

When the father clothed the son in a robe and placed a ring on his hand, the son was clearly restored to the position he had held before squandering it all. He did not return to a lower position. Though it took time for others to accept and recognize him, there was no waiting period for the father. The bringing forth of the calf and the feast shows a return to the father's provision. When we return to the Lord as our Shepherd, we leave the realm of lack (Psalm 23:1). His provision can supersede the law of sowing and reaping.

The elder son represents those people who have never fallen. They do not know what it means to be taken captive by sin. They do not know the shame and heartache of living with the past. Often they even despise God's goodness bestowed on the repentant sinner. It is easy for those who have never fallen to lose the whole point of the Gospel. Jesus came to seek and save that which was lost. This includes the backslidden Christian as well as the obstinate sinner.

Like this elder son, they are not receiving many of the blessings of the Father. Even though all He has is theirs, they do not experience it. They think the inheritance is a product of works. They serve God day and night, but not with joy. The idea of enjoying some of the blessings seems frivolous or beyond their reach. For this reason, they desire to see the repentant sinner suffer and live in a state of want. They want to see him suffer as his sins obviously deserve. They do not mind his being forgiven; they just do not want him restored.

If you have fallen, return to the Father. Let Him meet you with a kiss and restore you. If you are an elder brother, enter into the joy of the Lord. As you experience His goodness you may learn the power and peace of mercy. Let God make you a real peacemaker, as you proclaim the Gospel of peace to a world that believes He is an angry God.

# Twenty

## ❧

# Angry Preachers

# Twenty

## ❧

# *Angry Preachers*

*F*rom the earliest of times, angry men have misrepresented God. As ministers, we must realize that our opinions and emotions are not necessarily God's. Angry, judgmental preachers usually feel that "strong messages" will bring the people in line. But the Bible warns, *"Be...slow to speak, slow to wrath: for the wrath of man worketh not the righteousness of God"* (James 1:19–20). Many an angry preacher thought he was helping God out.

Hard words do not bring about repentance. They actually create new problems. The Bible says, *"Grievous words stir up anger"* (Proverbs 15:1). *"A wrathful man stirreth up strife"* (v. 18). *"The north wind driveth away rain* ["bringeth forth rain" in the original Hebrew]: *so doth an angry countenance* [bring forth] *a backbiting tongue"* (Proverbs 25:23). *"An angry man stirreth up strife"* (Proverbs 29:22). Hard preaching does not bring repentance; it brings rebellion. This is not my opinion; this is the Bible. When we ignore biblical principles of communication and instruction, we create problems. Angry preachers are like parents who gossip in front of their children, and then chastise them for having bad attitudes. When we criticize and judge from the pulpit, our people criticize and judge.

The only sure way to properly represent God is to walk in love. First John 4:12–13 says that when we walk in love, we dwell in God. The pulpit is not exempt from 1 Corinthians 13. We must preach with the same standards of communication as those required in daily life.

It is so important to understand the power of the minister. The way we relate to people is the way they assume God relates to them. Therefore, we dictate how they deal with sin. If we reject, they assume God rejects. If we restore and forgive, they believe God restores and forgives.

Several years ago I received a late-night call. A desperate voice on the other end asked me to come immediately to his home. I walked in to find a tear-stained face, overcome with shame and grief. This man was a dear friend. I was helping him to find his place in the ministry. But that night there was nothing but shame and despair.

As I sat down, he began to share a tale of perversion and sin. That night, it all came to a head. He felt he was over the edge. His secret sin had finally carried him to a point of destruction. After honestly confessing his sin to me, I asked him if he had confessed to God and asked Him for forgiveness. I shared a few words of encouragement and got up to leave. In utter amazement he asked, "Aren't you going to cast something out of me or deal with me?" The words sprang out of my heart, "You didn't sin against me; you sinned against God. If you've settled it with Him, it's settled with me. I don't discern a need for deliverance, but if you feel tempted, you take authority over it."

As I drove home I asked the Lord, "Did I say enough? Did I say the right things?" The Lord replied, "Because you showed him mercy, he was able to receive My mercy. Because you showed him love and acceptance, he was able to receive My love and acceptance."

Some years later, after I had gone through some personal destruction, I saw this man in a minister's conference. I went to talk with him. We talked briefly about the problems I had experienced. He gave me nothing but mercy and forgiveness. Then he said, "That night you came to my house, you saved my life." The way I related to him had given him confidence about the mercy of God.

Whatever you show a person is what he believes he will receive from the Lord. Be sure that you do not let your anger and disgust drive him from the mercy and grace he needs. Preachers are often overwhelmed by the sins of people. At times it seems that everyone is in sin. This can often overwhelm us to the point that we begin to pronounce judgment instead of peace.

Remember, everyone who comes to the doctor is sick. He does not turn against his patients because they are sick; he exists for the purpose of getting them well. I fear that our real ministerial motives are clearly revealed when we are merciless. Am I in the ministry to serve and heal hurting people, or am I using these people to build a ministry? We are here to serve the ones who are lost and the ones who backslide, as well as the ones who live godly lives.

It would be easy to become pessimistic and fearful. It would be easy to lose sight of the cures and focus on the sickness. But the doctor never reaches a place where he tries to destroy the patient; he tries to destroy the sickness. Likewise, we cannot destroy the people who are in the sin. The wrath of man will do that.

Fellowship with God is the only way they will be changed. If we drive them from God with a judgment message, we drive them from the only help available. *"But if we walk in the light, as he is in the light, we have fellowship one with another, and the blood of Jesus Christ his Son cleanseth us from all sin"* (1 John 1:7). They need the fellowship with Jesus in order to be cleansed from the power of the sin that is working in them.

Even Moses had a problem with being too judgmental. In Numbers 20:7–13, God told Moses how to represent Him before the people. Instead of speaking faith to the rock to bring forth water, he smote the rock twice. He was acting out of his anger with the people, but God was not. It was this sin that kept Moses out of the Promised Land.

Psalm 106:32–33 gives us some further insight: *"They angered him also at the waters of strife, so that it went ill with Moses for their sakes: because they provoked his spirit, so that he spake unadvisedly with his lips."* Because Moses was angry, he let his mouth get out of control. He displayed wrath instead of mercy.

Wrath always says God will kill you for this; mercy always says God will deliver you from this. Wrath is the product of frustration and unbelief. Proverbs 19:11 says, *"The discretion of a man deferreth his anger."* And Proverbs 14:29 says, *"He that is slow to wrath is of great understanding."* Unbelief does not see or believe that God is able to work in the situation. Understanding is calm because it believes the promises of God.

Moses learned that anger promotes foolishness and folly. *"He that is soon angry dealeth foolishly"* (v. 17). *"He that is hasty of spirit exalteth folly"* (v. 29). Our anger will lead us into a perversion of truth. After all, one of the root causes of anger in ministers is unforgiveness. We do not forgive those who hurt us, and we do not really want God to do so until they suffer. Anger for those who have sinned is also a form of gross self-righteousness. We fail to see the log in our eye because we are looking for the speck in theirs. We forget about our short-comings by focusing on theirs.

The smiting of the rock was like crucifying Christ afresh. Moses had already smitten the rock in the book of Exodus. The smiting of the rock brought water to an undeserving group of people. This time Moses displayed his feelings of anger and smote the rock again. This crucifying Christ afresh is the equivalent to pronouncing the judgment of God on those for whom Christ has already received judgment.

Shortly after I finished Bible college, a flood of judgment prophecies and books came forth. As I read these books, I began to take on that same spirit of destruction. I became angry with the people I once loved. Before, I had seen their potential. Now I saw their faults. Before, I believed God would change them. Now I wanted God to give them what they deserved. These books and prophecies offered no hope. It was too late for America and too late for the church. I will never forget the negative changes that came into my life from listening to these prophecies and reading these books.

Negative prophecies are self-fulfilling. They promote the fear and unbelief that it takes for them to come to pass. Proverbs 11:11 says, *"By the blessing of the upright the city is exalted: but it is overthrown by the mouth of the wicked."* We bless others when we speak good things. We curse others when we speak negatives. Jesus cursed the fig tree and it died. We curse our nation, our church, and our congregations by speaking negatives. Then they are brought to pass, but not by God. The fear and unbelief created by those words fulfill them.

Church members are often like children. Parents who have children who are emotionally disturbed are usually themselves faultfinding and critical. Preachers who should be building up are tearing down and destroying with their words of judgment. Finding fault does not make anyone more effective; it makes him introspective. When most people are in the presence of a faultfinder, they make more mistakes.

I have often heard it said, "I'm a prophet; therefore, I have a strong word." It is all right for it to be strong if it builds up. The New Testament guidelines for prophecy are edification, exhortation, and comfort (1 Corinthians 14:3). Let the Bible be the judge of the prophets of doom. Do their prophecies build up or tear down? Do they build faith or fear? Do they comfort or torment?

Ezekiel 13 warns against prophecy that comes out of your own heart. Verse 3 says, *"Woe unto the foolish prophets, that follow their own spirit, and have seen nothing!"* Let the New Testament measure of prophecy be the standard by which we judge all prophecy, and let these prophets of doom and gloom judge their own motivation.

First Timothy 1:5 says, *"Now the end* [goal] *of the commandment* [instruction] *is charity out of a pure heart, and of a good conscience, and of faith unfeigned."* We should understand the biblical goals of instruction. I want my teaching, preaching, and prophesying to bring a person to the place where he walks in love from a pure heart. I want him to have a conscience free from the pollutants of sin and guilt. I also want him to have a pure faith. That does not happen by promoting fear and rejection. Remember, every seed reproduces after its own kind.

What I sow from the pulpit is what I and the people will reap in the church and in our lives. If I am angry, I will breed anger. The anger I breed will be turned on me. If I criticize, I will produce criticism of me and the church. If I reject those who have faults, they will reject me when they see my faults.

I must get my own hurts healed so I can heal the hurting around me. I must be the one to whom people can come to see and experience the mercy and goodness of God.

# Twenty-one

&

# The Error of
# Balaam

# Twenty-one

## ଚ୍ଚ

# The Error of Balaam

hroughout church history there have been those
who desired to work their own agendas with God's
people. Some of them desire to use people for their
own personal gain. Many, on the other hand, desire to see
the church established, but because of ignorance or unbelief,
they do not trust the methods of God.

Do I believe God can change people by His Spirit when
they hear the truth? Or do I feel I must resort to carnal means
of fear and manipulation to accomplish the will of God? No
matter how I justify my actions, if I depart from biblical truth
to "help" someone, I am in sin.

When I received Jesus, the man who shared Scripture with
me was cursing and criticizing someone who had witnessed
to him. The Scripture he quoted was laced with profanity. It
came out of the mouth of a lost person. Yet, when I heard the
Word of God, the Holy Spirit had something to work with in
me. The Holy Spirit works with and confirms God's Word.

I am fully convinced that God can work with truth. We
need not resort to our frail and foolish attempts to bring men

to repentance. It seems that the most popular method of bringing people to repentance is the fear of judgment. We think we can scare people into returning to God. Fear may change one's actions, but only love will change one's heart.

The Bible warns against the error of Balaam and the way of Balaam. Now, these are not the same. They were sins committed by the same person, but they are different. We should know and avoid both of these sins. *"Woe unto them! for they have gone in the way of Cain, and ran greedily after the error of Balaam for reward, and perished in the gainsaying of Core"* (Jude 11). Lenski says Jude's warning has a climax: "taking the bad way (the way of Cain) which is to devote oneself to error, contradicting God's Word." They were willing to depart from God's Word because of what they had to gain. Let us examine this to understand how and why Balaam contradicted the Word of God.

Second Peter talks about the way of Balaam. The way of Balaam was to do unrighteousness for gain. This is a sin that is easy to detect. We are quick to label and deal with the one who uses the ministry for unrighteous profit. Yet there is a more deadly error that works among us. It brings more destruction and pain than the former, but it is considered to be acceptable. It also is the standard operating procedure for most Christians.

While Peter talked about the way of Balaam, Jude talked about the error of Balaam and associated it with Cain and Core. Balaam's error was to believe that God would curse what He had already blessed. He reasoned that since he was a prophet, if he spoke it, it would come about in truth. He tried to speak curses on God's people. Because he was motivated by greed, his greed caused him to justify his error.

It is easy for us to justify our actions when we enter the error of Balaam. Unlike Balaam, we are not doing it for greed.

Rather, we really want our friends, our family, or our church members to repent. We have a good motive, so the end justifies the means. But we are in sin, regardless of our motive, when we try to pronounce a curse on those whom God has blessed. Even if we think it will bring about repentance, it is sin.

It is even easier to justify when we see people change their behavior as a result of the fear we heap upon them. That type of change never lasts, however. In Christianity, people seem to cycle through life. They do pretty good, they get weary, they begin to compromise, they get into sin, they get miserable, and then they start the cycle all over again. Because they never come to have a meaningful relationship with God, their change is always short-lived. The fear that brought about repentance (an afterthought because of consequences) did not bring about real repentance (a change of mind).

The devil is a discourager. He always wants God's people to be cursed. Sadly, he is always able to find a willing soul to do his bidding. It is never too hard to find an angry, judgmental Christian who is ready to speak for God. In Numbers 22:12, God said to Balaam, *"Thou shalt not curse the people: for they are blessed."* How much more are the people of God blessed under this new covenant!

We have been set free from the curse, and no man, speaking by the Spirit, can pronounce the curse of God upon the people of God. In 1 Corinthians 12:3 we read, *"No man speaking by the Spirit of God calleth Jesus accursed."* We are the body of Christ. We are bone of His bone and flesh of His flesh. To pronounce judgment on God's people is to pronounce judgment on Jesus. Remember, when Paul persecuted the church, Jesus appeared to him and said, *"Saul, Saul, why persecutest thou me?"* (Acts 9:4, emphasis added). To persecute the church is to persecute Jesus. To pronounce judgment on the church is to pronounce judgment on Jesus.

In Christ, we have been delivered from condemnation. *"There is therefore now no condemnation to them which are in Christ Jesus, who walk not after the flesh, but after the Spirit"* (Romans 8:1). Condemnation is the expectation of judgment. Because we are free from the flesh (that is, righteousness by the works of the flesh), we don't have to live in fear of not "measuring up." We should not be living in the tormenting expectancy of judgment.

Because we have been reconciled (exchanged) and made righteous, we are delivered from wrath. *"Much more then, being now justified by his blood, we shall be saved from wrath through him"* (Romans 5:9).

Since judgment is totally contrary to the work of the cross, those who pronounce judgment are speaking contrary to the cross. The motive may be pure, but the belief is the error of Balaam. We should repent of our attempts to manipulate people into right behavior. Regardless of our motive, regardless of our logic, regardless of our theological preference, we must return to the truth. *"Or despisest thou the riches of his goodness and forbearance and longsuffering; not knowing that the goodness of God leadeth thee to repentance?"* (Romans 2:4).

Ironically, I have seen those who believe in grace and peace become as intolerant as anyone else. We must not attack, condemn, or judge those who preach a judgment message. At the same time, we must not entertain their words for a moment. As I stated earlier from Isaiah 54:17, *"Every tongue that riseth against thee in judgment, shalt thou prove to be lawless"* (RHM). We cannot accept the judgment message as valid or scriptural.

We must never see it as the attitude of God toward man. He has declared peace and goodwill toward men, through the Lord Jesus.

# Twenty-two

**જી**

# The Judgment of God

*Twenty-two*

ℬ

# The Judgment of God

O ne of the foundations of faith for the New Testament church is the doctrine of eternal judgment. Now, apart from knowing the truth about judgment, we could find ourselves in any one of many different types of error. But make no mistake, there will be a Day of Judgment. And that judgment will be far worse than anything being pronounced by the prophets of doom. It will be fierce, and it will be eternal.

The book of Revelation describes with vivid detail that time when the wrath of God will be poured out on the world. Even then we, the church, will be delivered from His wrath. John wrote, *"I was in the Spirit on the Lord's day"* (Revelation 1:10). *"The Lord's day"* refers to that great and terrible Day (period of time) when the judgment of God will come upon the earth. All the events in the book of Revelation take place at that time.

It is worthy to note, however, that even this fierce judgment does not bring repentance. *"Neither repented they of their murders, nor of their sorceries, nor of their fornication, nor of their thefts"* (Revelation 9:21). Judgment, regardless of how severe, does not bring repentance.

When unredeemed man stands before God, it will be in the Great White Throne Judgment. Those who have not accepted Jesus as their righteousness will appear before God to be judged according to their works (Revelation 20:12). They will be judged according to their works because that is the only righteousness they will have. They will have rejected the free gift of righteousness in Jesus. But, unfortunately, *"by the deeds of the law there shall no flesh be justified in his sight: for by the law is the knowledge of sin"* (Romans 3:20). To stand before God, having rejected the righteousness of Jesus, will always mean an eternal hell.

The Bible says God will judge in righteousness. It is righteous to judge a world that has rejected the free gift of righteousness. Jesus suffered sin, the curse, hell, and torment for all the world. No man needs to suffer hell. It is total and absolute defiance for a man to reject such a great and merciful salvation. Righteousness demands the judgment of these people. These people will not be judged as to salvation; they already had that opportunity. They will be judged by their works in which they trusted.

With the absolute certainty of this future judgment, we should proclaim that God's mercy is available now. Pointing out a future judgment is not bad, if you give people the Good News as well. The Good News is this: You do not have to be judged. You do not have to go to hell. Jesus has paid the price. You can have the free gift of righteousness.

The believer will never come into the White Throne Judgment. The believer will appear before the judgment seat of Christ. Second Corinthians 5:10 says, *"For we must all appear before the judgment seat of Christ; that every one may receive the things done in his body, according to that he hath done, whether it be good or bad."*

Does this mean, as some say, that we will all stand before Jesus and have our every past sin exposed? I think not. Most of the Scriptures used to support that view are taken out of context.

I am not sure how this will happen, but all our works will pass through the fire before appearing before the Lord. *"Every man's work shall be made manifest: for the day shall declare it, because it shall be revealed by fire; and the fire shall try every man's works of what sort it is"* (1 Corinthians 3:13). The fire will test our works to determine if they are wood, hay, stubble, or precious metals.

Works that are based on the foundation of faith-righteousness are good works. We are called to good works in Christ Jesus. We have a purpose in this life: We should bear fruit. Dead works, on the other hand, are those things we do to make ourselves righteous and acceptable before God. Those dead works will be burned. They are a testimony to our unbelief in the finished work of Jesus. But even if all our works are burned, we will be saved. *"If any man's work shall be burned, he shall suffer loss: but he himself shall be saved; yet so as by fire"* (v. 15).

The real purpose for our standing before the Lord is to receive rewards. First Corinthians 3:14 says, *"If any man's work abide which he hath built thereupon, he shall receive a reward."* There will be wonderful rewards for what we have done in this life in response to the goodness of God. There is much I do not understand about this time of rewards. I dare not even speculate, but I know it will be glorious.

Although people should know about the eternal judgments of the Great White Throne Judgment, they also should know about the judgment seat of Christ, where our works will be judged and we will be given rewards. Since there will be these judgments, let us judge our own motives. Let us live, walk, and minister in the love of God so we will receive our reward. Let us minister in a way that glorifies Jesus instead of man.

Because there will be a Day of Judgment, let us preach, teach, and warn men everywhere to turn from wickedness. But let's do it in love and goodness, which bring men to repentance.

Let us not despise the lost and the backslidden, but let us, with mercy and kindness, restore them to the Lord. Let us have the same value for the human race as God did when He sacrificed His Son to reconcile the world to Himself. Let them taste and see that the Lord is good when they experience (taste) God through us. If God is at peace with the world through Jesus, then we, as His ambassadors, should be at peace.

Let us refrain from breeding fear and living in fear. Fear is not from God. Fear causes people to run from a loving Father into an eternal destruction. As Revelation 21:8 says, *"But the fearful, and unbelieving...shall have their part in the lake which burneth with fire and brimstone: which is the second death."* Of all the sins that would enslave a man, fear and unbelief are at the top of the list.

Fear prevents you from believing and trusting the God who loves you and freely gives you the gift of righteousness in Jesus. We should understand the reality of the judgment that Jesus received in our place when He went to the cross. We should be confident that we do not have to fear judgment in this life.

Twenty-three

&

# The Need for Peace

*Twenty-three*

દ૪

# *The Need for Peace*

*I*n my early days of ministry, I put a strong emphasis on meeting the physical needs of people. I have always had great compassion for people who are hurting. Because of my struggles with sickness, I understood the suffering of people in physical pain. Motivated by compassion, I saw many wonderful miracles. As I have traveled around the world, I have seen every miracle in the New Testament. I have seen many of them hundreds of times.

Although I still place a high value on the physical needs of man, I now see the emotional/spiritual needs to be far more essential than the physical. As a matter of fact, when the emotional needs are met, it is relatively easy to take care of the physical needs. But the emotional needs of a person are met only through personally experiencing the love of God through the Lord Jesus Christ.

People need to feel the love and peace of God. We all need to be permeated with the positive emotions that come from a meaningful relationship with God. We can endure sickness, poverty, and pain, but we cannot endure poverty of the inner man. Proverbs 18:14 says it this way: *"The spirit of a man will sustain his infirmity; but a wounded spirit who can bear?"*

Physical healing is meaningless to the person who has a broken heart. Prosperity does not ease the pain of loneliness. Success is no substitute for a sense of dignity and worth that comes from the Lord Jesus. We do not want to deny God's desire and willingness to meet the physical needs, but we must bring it into perspective.

God created man. He placed him in a garden called Paradise. There was no pain, suffering, or sorrow. Man lived in a peaceful, loving relationship with God. That is the environment for which we were created. We were never designed to live apart from peace, love, and acceptance.

The day Adam ate the forbidden fruit, he acquired a new capacity for the human race: the knowledge of good and evil. With this knowledge, man now started making decisions about good and evil independently of God. Man began to determine righteousness apart from God. Subsequently, he rejected God's standards and developed his own. Hence, we have the birth of religion.

Religion has always been mean, and it is still mean. The first religion is the same as it has always been. It is man attempting to relate to God on his own terms. In order to do that we must, of course, reject God's terms. We also must reject anyone who does not comply to our terms.

The first religion caused Cain to kill Abel. He hated him because Abel's sacrifice was accepted and his wasn't. He had labored for his sacrifice. Logic would say that his was of more value, but Cain was operating in his own knowledge of righteousness and unrighteousness. *"Cain...slew his brother. And wherefore slew he him? Because his own works were evil, and his brother's righteous"* (1 John 3:12).

Thousands of years later, Paul said in the book of Galatians that the children of the flesh always persecute the children of the Spirit. In other words, the religious always persecute the righteous. Why? The religious despise the righteousness that God has chosen and given.

There is a logic to religion. Religion is man's attempt to be right with God and find peace in a way that makes sense to him. Religion sees the greatest need of man as being right. To the religious logic, being right is equivalent to being right with God. If someone doesn't agree with us, he is implying that we are wrong.

Since it is essential that we be right, we must prove him wrong. If we can't prove him wrong, then we kill him. That's exactly what Cain did. The need to be right has tormented men since the day Adam ate the fruit. Adam started making decisions apart from God right off the bat. "We had better make some clothes to cover ourselves, because I don't think it's right to be naked before God. We had better hide when God calls us. He's probably mad." Man began to scramble to be right. But every decision to be right, apart from God's perspective, drove him deeper into pain, suffering, and a self-imposed separation from God.

Regardless of how pure the motives, regardless of how sincere the intention, regardless of the dedication to God, regardless of how good we are, the attempt to establish right and wrong apart from God is a rejection of God and His truth. *"For they being ignorant of God's righteousness, and going about to establish their own righteousness, have not submitted themselves unto the righteousness of God"* (Romans 10:3).

Every attempt at being righteous with God apart from accepting His terms ultimately will have a negative effect. As long as we're doing everything right, we will have peace, but when we fail, we will lose peace. There will never be an abiding sense of confidence and peace—one that lasts despite our success or failure. The Bible says that law cannot make one righteous; it can only give him an awareness of sin. So when you fail you will no longer have peace.

Then there is the problem of those who disagree with us. They have a different definition of *righteous* than we have. We must prove them wrong in order to maintain our peace. The struggle is endless. You cannot live this way. You were not created to live this way.

God wants you to live in a harmonious relationship with Him and in harmonious relationships with people. This can happen only when you have peace. You can have peace only when you know you are righteous. You can know you are righteous only when you accept the gift of righteousness through the Lord Jesus Christ. Romans 5:1 says it best: *"Therefore being justified* [made righteous] *by faith, we have peace with God through our Lord Jesus Christ."*

Peace is far more essential to Christian living than we have ever realized. The gift of righteousness produces peace through Jesus. Peace gives boldness and confidence to pursue a relationship with God. Through Him we have access to grace (God's ability) in which we stand. When there is no peace, there will be no relationship, no confidence, and no grace to work in our lives. And apart from grace we are limited to our own ability to serve God and live a righteous life. We need peace!

Twenty-four

&

# More than a State of Mind

*Twenty-four*

**৪০**

# More than a State of Mind

There are many things a person can do to have a tranquil state of mind. There is nothing wrong with many of those things. But tranquility apart from reality (truth) is a deception. If you convince yourself that there is no God, you can gain a certain degree of tranquility. It may work in this life, but it will fail the test of eternity.

There are many things of which an individual could convince himself. If you believe there is no hell, it could bring you peace while you reject God. But that is not a reality. If you convince yourself that God loves you because you live right, that will produce peace as long as you live right. Again, that is not a reality.

God's peace is based on a reality. It is based on the uncompromising, unfailing love of God that was demonstrated at the cross of Christ. Only by knowing and believing the message of the cross will you find a peace that abides. It does not fluctuate with circumstances. It is not based on a lie.

When one believes the truth, the Holy Spirit is able to perform that truth and shed the love of God abroad in his heart.

It is the reality or unreality you believe that becomes the reality you experience. The apostle John said it this way: *"And we have known and believed the love that God hath to us. God is love; and he that dwelleth in love dwelleth in God, and God in him"* (1 John 4:16).

The Greek word for *know* speaks of an experiential knowledge. To experience the love of God, you must first believe the love of God. The love of God can be realized only by what He did at the cross.

> *In this was manifested the love of God toward us, because that God sent his only begotten Son into the world, that we might live through him. Herein is love, not that we loved God, but that he loved us, and sent his Son to be the propitiation for our sins.* (1 John 4:9–10)

The reality that Jesus came into the world, took our sins, and appeased the wrath of God (as our propitiation) clearly demonstrates the love of God. The knowledge of being delivered from wrath causes us to realize His love. The knowledge of being made righteous causes us to experience His peace. No sedative, no sin, nothing can provide the tranquility and fulfillment that comes from experiencing and abiding in the love and peace of God.

God made peace with you through the cross. Will you accept that peace? It may be time for you to pray a prayer similar to the following:

> Father, today I choose to believe truth. You sent Jesus into this world; He became my sin; He took my punishment; He went to hell in my place. He came out of the grave and conquered my sin. In Him I have the gift of righteousness. I thank You that I am righteous apart from my performance. Today I acknowledge that You have never hurt me. You are not judging me. You are not

the source of pain in my life. My own sin and unbelief have brought me pain. I will never again believe that You are hurting me. I will abide in Your peace because I am righteous in Jesus! You love me; You accept me; You are with me. You have made me accepted in the Beloved!

॰ৎ

# About the Author

# About the Author

એ

Almost thirty years ago, James Richards found Jesus and answered the call to ministry. His dramatic conversion and passion to help hurting people launched him onto the streets of Huntsville, Alabama. His mission was to reach teenagers and drug abusers.

Before his salvation, James was a professional musician with all the trappings of a worldly lifestyle. More than anything, he was searching for real freedom. Sick of himself and his empty pursuits, he hated all that his life had become. He turned to drugs as a means of escape and relief. Although he was desperate to find God, his emotional outrage made people afraid to tell him about Jesus. He sought help but became more confused and hopeless than before. He heard much religious talk, but not the life-changing Gospel.

Through a miraculous encounter with God, James Richards gave his life to the Lord and was set free from his addictions. His whole life changed! Now, after years of ministry, Dr. Richards still believes there's no one God can't help, and there's no one God doesn't love. He has committed his life to helping people experience that love. If his life is a model for anything, it is that God never quits on anyone.

Dr. Richards—author, teacher, theologian, counselor, and businessman—is president and founder of Impact Ministries, a multifaceted, international ministry committed to helping those whom the church has not yet reached. He is on the cutting edge of what works in today's society. He is president and founder of Impact International School of Ministry, Impact International Fellowship of Ministers, Impact Treatment Center, Impact of Huntsville Church, and Impact International Publications. Thousands have been saved, healed, and delivered every year through his worldwide crusades and pastors' seminars.

With doctorates in theology, human behavior, and alternative medicine, and an honorary doctorate in world evangelism, Dr. Richards is also a certified detox specialist and drug counselor, as well as a trainer for the National Acupuncture Detoxification Association (NADA). His uncompromising yet positive approach to the Gospel strengthens, instructs, and challenges people to new levels of victory, power, and service. Dr. Richards' extensive experience in working with substance abuse, codependency, and other social/emotional issues has led him to pioneer effective, creative, Bible-based approaches to ministry that meet the needs of today's world.

More than anything else, Dr. Richards believes that people need to be made whole by experiencing God's unconditional love. His message is simple, practical, and powerful. His passion is to change the way the world sees God so that they can experience a relationship with Him through Jesus.

He and his wife, Brenda, have five daughters and nine grandchildren and reside in Huntsville, Alabama.

# Bibliography

Bromiley, Geoffrey. *The Theological Dictionary of the New Testament.* Edited by Gerhard Kittel and Gerhard Friedrich. Grand Rapids: Wm. B. Eerdmans, 1985.

Cremer, Hermann. *Biblico-Theological Lexicon of New Testament Greek.* Edinburgh: T&T Clark, 1895.

Lenski, Richard C. *The Interpretation of St. Paul's Epistle to the Romans.* Minneapolis, Minn.: Augsburg Fortress, 1936.

McIntosh and Twyman, trans. *The Archko Volume, or the Archeological Writings of the Sanhedrin and Talmuds of the Jews.* New York: McGraw Hill, 2000.

Richards, Dr. James B. *Grace: The Power to Change.* New Kensington, Pa.: Whitaker House, 2001.

———. *Taking the Limits Off God.* Huntsville, Ala.: Impact Ministries, 1989.

Strong, James, ed. *The New Strong's Exhaustive Concordance of the Bible.* Nashville: Thomas Nelson, 1997.

Thayer, Joseph H. *Thayer's Greek-English Lexicon of the New Testament.* Peabody, Mass.: Hendrickson Publishers, 1997.

Tregelles, Samuel Prideaux, LL.D. *Gesenius' Hebrew-Chaldee Lexicon to the Old Testament.* Grand Rapids: Baker Book House, 1979.

Trench, Richard Chenevix. *Trench's Synonyms of the New Testament.* Peabody, Mass.: Hendrickson Publishers, 2000.

Vaughan, Curtis, ed. *The Bible from 26 Translations.* Grand Rapids: Baker Book House, 1989.

# ANOTHER POWERFUL *B*OOK
## from Whitaker House

**Grace: The Power to Change**

*Dr. James B. Richards*

Christians everywhere have been missing the truth about grace—and living in defeat as a result. Grace is God's ability working in you to do what you cannot. It is the power to change. Take to heart the principles in this book, and discover the dimension of Christian living that Jesus called "easy and light." Jesus has finished the work, so relax and let His grace change your heart!

ISBN: 0-88368-730-5 • Trade • 192 pages

# ANOTHER POWERFUL BOOK
## from Whitaker House

### Make Fear Bow
*Dr. Gary V. Whetstone*

So many times you've tried to talk yourself out of the terror that gnaws within, but it hasn't worked. You're riddled with tension and guilt. You try to move forward, but unseen fears lurk around every corner, causing you to imagine the worst. You're frozen in your tracks, held captive by fear. But life doesn't have to be this way. You can live in confidence and peace. Using time-tested biblical principles, you can conquer your fears and walk in freedom. Dr. Gary Whetstone shows you how to *Make Fear Bow* today!

ISBN: 0-88368-776-3 • Trade • 272 pages

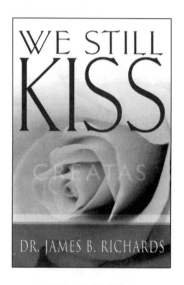